girl walks into a bar

girl walks into a bar

a memoir

strawberry saroyan

random house new york

"Twelfth, Between A & B," was previously published in *Personals: Dreams and Nightmares from the Lives of Twenty Young Writers* (New York: Houghton Mifflin, 1998), Thomas Beller, ed.

Grateful acknowledgment is made to the following for permission to reprint previously published material:

Q PRIME MANAGEMENT: Excerpt from "Seether" (1994) written by Nina Gordon and performed by Veruca Salt. Copyright © 1994 by Are You There God, It's Me Music (ASCAP). Reprinted by permission.

SPECIAL RIDER MUSIC: Excerpt from "Shooting Star" by Bob Dylan. Copyright © 1989 by Special Rider Music. All rights reserved. International copyright secured. Reprinted by permission.

LIBRARY OF CONGRESS CATALOGING-IN-PUBLICATION DATA
Saroyan, Strawberry.
   Girl walks into a bar: a memoir / Strawberry Saroyan.
      p.   cm.
   ISBN 0-375-50611-X
   1. Saroyan, Strawberry. 2. Journalists—United States—Biography. I. Title.
   PN4874.S27 A3 2003
   070.92—dc21
   [B]
                                                      2002036759

Printed in the United States of America on acid-free paper

Random House website address: www.randomhouse.com

9 8 7 6 5 4 3 2

First Edition

Book design by Casey Hampton

to all the other girls out there,

wandering these same streets

contents

girl walks into a bar

twelfth, between a & b

I t's hard to say when my virginity became something that I wanted to lose. At eighteen, I remember, I couldn't have cared less about it. I was waiting for love, and when my blond surfer date asked me so sweetly one night to stay over in his dorm room, I had no trouble saying no. Maybe in a few weeks, if we were in love, I would tease him—then I would, perhaps, but not now, no way, sorry honey, I would say.

But the surfer and I didn't last that long and, over the years, no one else seemed to either. My know-how in the dating department ended after round one: I had no problem choosing a guy I liked and silently, almost magically, seducing him into holding my hand and kissing me and making out with me at a party or in the woods or in my bed. But I could take it no further. The next day, I would feel ashamed and embarrassed by my behavior. "What was I thinking last night? My God, I was really drunk," I would say to my friends and laugh, trying to sound as though it didn't matter. The next time I saw the guy, I would act as if nothing had happened, act tough and untouchable.

Inside, I would simply feel a blackness, an emptiness that seemed so big it was impossible to get through. The few times I had tried to explore it, I'd stopped when I'd started to feel like I was drowning. I was, quite simply, terrified. My terror wasn't so much of sex per se (although that was part of it) but, I think now, more of the sensation of not knowing what I was getting into with these guys, of confusion itself. And during this time, these years, I believed that the ones who didn't call or try to see me again, I liked, and the ones who liked me, I didn't. It was funny how it always seemed to happen that way and it was also somehow a horrible relief.

So I came to be, at twenty-five, still a virgin. While my friends had been having their first relationships, if not yet their first loves, I had spent my late teens and early twenties retreating into a series of infatuations. These infatuations demanded little of me, yet they supplied me with an endless well of feelings to draw upon at any time. I would spend months upon months in a safe cocoon of thoughts about someone I might have spent only one (chaste) night with, or gone out with just two or three times. I could pull these men, and the little things I remembered about them, out like cards at opportune moments, when I needed a pick-me-up or felt like a dash of emotion. The way he used to flick his hair, the way he used to say my name, the way he used to kiss me; I would replay these details over and over, and live on them, use them as touchstones to brighten up my day in a bittersweet way.

I spoke to two or three girlfriends about my virginity, but otherwise no one knew my secret. To most people, I was just another sophisticated young Manhattanite, drinking my gin and tonics and reading my Mary McCarthy and perfecting my ice-cool take on the world. But I was beginning to feel left out. The friends whom I did tell didn't seem to understand my problem. Why didn't I simply go out and sleep with someone? they would ask, vaguely patronizing me, I thought. After all, guys will sleep with anyone, it's not that hard to get them into bed, and I was attractive and smart, anyway, they would say. One night I had finally tried to just go out and do it, but I couldn't figure out quite how to broach the topic with the male friend whom I had hesitantly selected to be my "first." I was too shy to propose that we just go back to his place and go to bed together. But it was also more than that: I felt paralyzed to help myself out of this problem, for reasons I could not, and still do not, particularly understand. Because not having sex was never about religion or morality for me, although at first it was a little bit about love. But even that, at a certain point, fell by the wayside.

So it's hard to say exactly when it happened, but gradually my virginity became an important entity in my life. It began to dictate my decisions, to distort my sense of myself, and, in the end, to become a constant, droning, hopeless backdrop against which everything else occurred. And it became all of these things in the form of a voice, a voice that said I was never going to have sex because there was something fatally flawed in me and that I might as well just face it.

During the five years I lived in New York, I dated maybe ten men in all. Most of the time, I was not particularly unhappy about this. I thought that I didn't go out with that many men because I knew what I wanted. For the life of me now, however, I cannot recall exactly what that was. I can say that I had a vague fantasy about being part of a media "power couple" (I was starting out as a journalist), and that my ideal mix included fame, money, and eccentricity. I also liked womanizers, because they made it easy for me. I was nervous, and their often outrageous come-ons both distracted me and let me off the hook from having to initiate anything. My only job was to say no.

I could go on about the men I met who measured up to some or all of my fantasy, but the truth is that the minutiae of many of my encounters aren't that interesting. Most of them start to seem the same in retrospect, even to me, although when they were taking place each word, each look weighed heavily. That is what makes them seem the same, in the end: They were all too important.

I think the more interesting story, the real story, is what was happening to me without them, or without someone, in my life. These were the years between twenty and twenty-five for me, and they coincided with the years that I lived in New York City, and the years in which I began to grow up.

One afternoon, during the first term of my sophomore year at a small liberal arts college in Portland, Oregon, I got a call from my father. He'd had a fight with my grandmother, he said, and subsequently received a letter from her saying that she would

twelfth, between a & b 7

no longer be paying for my college education, and that none of us were to contact her.

I'd always suspected rejection might be just around the corner with my grandmother, from the days that I had gone as a hippie child to visit her in her big house in Los Angeles and driven around with her in her Rolls-Royce. I had always felt that somehow my family and I never quite measured up to her expectations or quite fit into her life, and what my father told me on the phone that day seemed proof of this. As we talked, I felt numb, and then panicked. The financial implications of this fight were real and immediate; I had just a few thousand dollars of my own in savings, and my parents were both freelance artists with little money.

Over the next several days, however, I came up with a plan. I would have to transfer to a better college (no one would be there to catch my fall anymore, I realized, and I needed to get a degree that would mean something to the outside world), I would have to get a sizable scholarship to attend this new college, and, in order to do that, I would need to get straight A's for the rest of the year. I decided that I would transfer to a school in New York City. I am not entirely sure why I chose New York, but having just come back from a term "abroad" there, it occurs to me that being in the eye of this crisis may have subconsciously reminded me of being in the city. Manhattan is, after all, the only place I know of that moves at the speed of panic.

So I escaped my emotional predicament for the rest of the academic year by working nonstop. I had just gotten my first journalism assignment and I added that to my full course load, which I attacked with a zeal bordering on compulsion. I began to brew a strong pot of coffee for myself every night at midnight, and to drink it all to keep myself going until around two. I started running every day, and recall one evening after I'd been working out for over an hour, a friend of mine remarked with concern that I looked white as a sheet. I stopped fooling around with men because I didn't have the time. In April, I was accepted by Barnard for the following fall, and received better financial aid than I had dared to hope for.

I arrived in Manhattan one hot September day in 1990. It is hard to describe what a relief the city was to me then. The noise, the activity, the skyscrapers, the concrete—it all felt oddly natural, and it made me happy for the first time in what seemed like years. I was suspicious of the happiness, though, because it had been so long since I'd felt anything like it. I confided to several friends that I thought I might get run over by a car because things were finally going well for me.

Things were not going so well for the rest of my family, though, and during my first months in the city, I felt under increasing pressure to succeed on their behalf as well as mine. Recently, my parents had both had to get regular jobs for the first time in their lives, and they'd started at the bottom. My mother had begun working in retail at the local suburban mall, and my father, among other things, was driving an airport van. That summer, my brother and sister, both younger, had been admitted to a drug rehab hospital for teenagers. They remained there as I began my first term at Barnard. I felt, as I remarked to a friend as we sat on the steps at Columbia one afternoon, that I was the "hope of the family."

I spent the bulk of my time at Barnard either in class or studying in my dorm room. Working hard there felt more like a game than a chore to me, though, and for the most part I enjoyed myself. I had always been a good student, but never before had I been around so many other people who were also high achievers. I saw myself in my fellow students and it made me aware of my own worth, gave me a sense of momentum and pride that I had never experienced before. I was happy, and safe, in my little world.

Graduating, then, was like being taken out of a scale model of life and suddenly being told to run around and figure out the real thing. I had one experience in particular that first June that overwhelmed me and made me nervous about the prospect of becoming involved with someone. One night I went to a party in the East Village and met a guy who struck me as being perfect. He looked perfect (a blonde again, very Waspy, from the perfectly-glamorous-but-perfectly-wholesome-sounding city of Champaign, Illinois), he had the perfect job (he was an editor, something that I hoped to soon become—although he worked in books, and I wanted to work in magazines), and he also seemed to like me. All night, with an unwavering stare and an ironic smile, he complimented me on specific parts of my body: my eyelashes, my shoulders, my ass—"the ass of a twenty-one-year-old," he called it. I thought it was a little crude but I forgave him, because no matter what he said it was all framed by his air of impossible flawlessness, his sparkly smile and effortless grace, his eyes like little windows.

As the party wound down, I decided to leave, and the perfect guy asked if he could come with me. Together we walked to a nearby bar and sat down at a table in the back. Then, out of nowhere, he said that he had to know when I had lost my virginity. It was important to him; it was important to our "relationship," he said with a smile. And I looked at him, and I lied. I told him that I'd been twelve. He was a little surprised I'd been so young, he said, but he understood. I was probably from one of those liberal academic families, and my parents were probably professors, and I had started early simply out of a lack of midwestern guilt and all of that crap, hadn't I? he said. And I just nodded.

Almost immediately, though, I had to come clean. I had never told a guy I was a virgin before so I didn't know what to expect, but after I said it I felt as if I had opened up the floodgates to about a million other things to say and explain and do. It made no difference that his reaction wasn't particularly dramatic (I dimly recall a mixture of mild surprise and amusement)—regardless, I was suddenly a wreck. I excused myself and went to the bathroom. When I came back, I told him that I wanted to go home, that I just felt exposed, like he didn't think I was sexy anymore. I told him that I knew he'd just wanted to go to bed with some girl tonight and now he was stuck with this goddamn novice, and I told him that I was sorry. And then he kissed me and said that that was what he liked about me, that I was innocent and sophisticated at the same time. Then he took me home with him.

We didn't do much that night in the way of sex (just my usual above-the-waist make-out drill), and we didn't do much any other night either. As usual, it ended after about two weeks, during which time I spent the night twice. But what was different about my interaction with this guy was that he knew that I was a virgin—and not only did he know, but he seemed okay with it. One morning, though, after he'd been teasing me about my impressive resistance to his overwhelming charms, I casually said that maybe we should have sex. I had hoped he might be flattered. Instead, he said, "Oh, we can't have sex, because then you'll fall in love with me." That was what he said. But what I heard was that he didn't want me to fall in love with him. And what that meant to my twenty-one-year-old virginal self was that *he* didn't want to, or just plain wasn't going to, fall in love with *me*. And I felt the familiar blackness again, but I just acted as though everything were fine, and then I left.

That fall, my college roommate Natasha and I moved into a little apartment downtown. To pay my rent, I spent my days temping at a bank in Brooklyn, but I hoped to soon land a job on staff at a magazine. It was difficult. Until the end of that year, I interviewed for a good number of positions, but I failed to land even the most mundane (among them, a writing position at an encyclopedia company, for which I was asked to prepare a writing sample that was completely devoid of a personal voice).

During this time, Natasha and I lived as though we were perpetually at camp. We had no furniture, and we ate a lot of Chinese takeout and a frozen dessert called Tasti D•Lite, and we watched a lot of David Letterman. We didn't realize it at first, but it gradually dawned on us that we had no friends. Everyone we'd known at school had left the city, and beyond a few stray people—family friends, distant relatives—we were completely alone. For my birthday that October, Natasha came home with a Ben & Jerry's Brownie Bar, a box of cake candles, and a Madonna CD for me. After our little celebration, I took a walk alone and contemplated my life. It wasn't what I had pictured it would be. I was in New York, after all: Where *was* everybody?

In January, I was hired to be the assistant to the editor in chief of a glossy magazine. I was excited and intimidated by my new job, which plunged me into the upper echelons of the publishing world. Suddenly, I was speaking with the movers and shakers I'd only read about before, and it felt glamorous, even if it was just to put them through to my boss. I applied myself with unusual enthusiasm to all of my tasks, from making lunch reservations with an impeccable combination of reserve and presumption, to sorting through the mail with an eagle eye to what was, and wasn't, a priority. During the entire first year I am aware of having made just one mistake, which I immediately rectified; I was, in short, a great assistant. Yet during my first six months at this job, I became increasingly sure that my boss didn't like me, and I prepared myself on a daily basis for my imminent firing. There was, I was certain, something outside my sphere of vision, something intangible, that made me unacceptable. The horrible beauty of this thing, of course, was that I couldn't identify it. There was nothing that I could do to solve a problem I couldn't see.

It was only gradually, over the course of days and months and even into my second year at the magazine, that I began to see that I was wrong. My boss, I realized, was kind. He didn't say much or show much, but he was looking out for me. He encouraged my writing and editing, and, after the first year or so, he promoted me to a position that involved more creative tasks—and he promoted me again several times thereafter. He never told me I was talented (until he wrote it on my farewell card), but he was one of the first people who made me feel that way.

Socially, things also began to open up. It was around this time that I met a group of young writers through another assistant and began to tap into a social scene. I started going to this group's parties, reading the books they read and the pieces they wrote, wearing a lot of black, and making the kind of cutting observations that made them seem so cool. The curious thing was, most of them were men—all vaguely my type—but it rarely even crossed my mind to become involved with any of them. Of course, I could say that I was still obsessing over the blond editor (and I was) and that they were professional contacts (and they were—and, my logic went, why risk alienating a perfectly good professional contact?). There was also, however, something about the way that I related to these guys that I couldn't quite put my finger on at the time, but which made them seem off-limits to me. It was, I think now, that I knew them for what became finally years, and yet I never had an actual conversation with any of them. We liked being around each other because it looked good on the outside, but there was very little actually going on between us.

In the end, I did attempt a romance with one of these men. He was the one I met last, and he was different than the rest in that he was both more extreme and more obviously vulnerable. He had a drug problem and could often be found at the end of the evening, after the party was over, in a semi-conscious stupor. Then one of the others would take it upon himself to make sure he made it home safely. His apartment was massive. The first time I went to a party there, I described it to people afterward as being the size of an airport hangar. I had never seen anything like it in the city, except in museums. Fascinated by who he might be, I ducked into his office one night and came upon a piece of his writing. Of course, I immediately recognized it as a work of brilliance. He was the real writer of them all, I thought to myself. And gradually, without my even speaking to him really, the combination of his tremendous wealth yet obvious unhappiness, his need for help, his distractedness (he was so drunk that perhaps he wouldn't notice how screwed up I was), his talent, his prep-school clothes even, began to work on me, until they coalesced into a fantasy of our ending up together. And then one night before heading off to another party at his place, I decided I would try to make it come true.

I got dressed like a mod schoolgirl in Mary Janes and a short black pleated skirt and set off on my mission. It went well. We talked for the first time by the pool table early on, and then he kept seeking me out all night with discreet little gestures—purposely bumping into me, or giving me a smile in an off moment. The next morning, he called: Did I want to go to a rock show with him that evening?

I did, of course, and the beginning of our date was suitably madcap—we bought counterfeit tickets, so had to run past the guards—but as the evening wore on, I began to feel the familiar sensation of the date's promise slipping away from me. We ended up going to a series of crowded trendy bars and engaging in stilted conversation. As the hours ticked by, I became increasingly combative, hoping that he might think it was sexy or intriguing. While he was walking me home at the end of the night, after an awkward silence, he said, "You're not really a hippie-type girl, are you?" I realized then that that had been his fantasy of me, and I hadn't measured up. We kissed politely at my door, and for the next few days, I had the sensation that I was almost floating I liked him so much, but I also suspected that I wouldn't hear from him again. When he never did call, I began plotting my revenge. The next time I saw him at a party, I would walk right up to him with a glass full of champagne and crush it in his face.

What strikes me most about this date now is the fantasy element. Of course, fantasy exists in most romance, but I think it is particularly encouraged and intensified in all aspects of one's life in New York. To live in the city almost demands it, for why else would so many people put up with so little space, such high prices, such bitter winters, such feverish summers? Why else would I have slept in a room that could barely fit a bed for years, still just narrowly surviving on a salary that allowed me to buy nothing more than food and clothes? I did it because my real life, somehow, wasn't actually my real life in New York. My real life was my fantasy life, and it would start in, say, five years, maybe less, when I was a big success—when I was rich, or famous, or both.

It's easy to stay in touch with the fantasy in New York,

where money, glamour, and fame are almost palpable on the street. Most days, I experienced elements of it—being enveloped by the whiff of cash at Barneys, for example, or the glare of flashbulbs at a fashion show, or, on my way home from work, walking past a movie star on the street. Constantly experiencing the fantasy, or being reminded of it, kept me focused on attaining it. And it was fun for a while.

But it was also confusing. It began to cause me and, I think, the men I knew too, to relate to people according to a fantasy of who they might be instead of getting to know who they actually were. It caused us to conduct our lives, and our relationships, as though we were writing scripts, or starring in them. I did it, and I had it done to me. How else can I explain the combination of glamorous gestures but total lack of substance in my love life in New York, a city where I had men buy me Raymond Chandler novels and send me letters quoting poets, a city where men took my high heels off at parties and nibbled my toes, where millionaires arrived at my apartment for dates without wallets, and men told me, in casual conversation, that they were going to spank me if I wasn't good? How else can I explain these moments—all of which were ostensibly in the service of romance, but which never led to any real romance—except to say that they actually had little to do with anything, barring the fact that they sounded like they would make a good story later, both to these men and to me, and that that is why we were attracted to each other in the first place? We both spoke the language of fantasy.

As Natasha and I used to say: Good anecdote, bad reality; that was what my life became. Because the truth of it was that

I met a few men in New York who were straightforward, who liked me, who were smart and nice and funny and available, but I didn't want them. I didn't want them because they were too accessible. They were too real.

Of course, to be with these fantasy men, one must be a fantasy oneself. And so I took on playing the different roles and dressing the different parts of who I wanted to be, or who I thought various men wanted me to be. Much of it, I enjoyed. I was the right age for experimenting with my identity, and with my clothes and hair and makeup. But sometimes the illusion snuck up on and startled me and made me uncomfortable. I would find myself whispering to a guy for no reason, for example, or becoming very conscious of the way I was chewing my food across the table from a date, or trying to give a man the kind of undivided attention that I had read was Jackie Kennedy's secret, or pretending that I'd read a book when I hadn't, just to make some guy think I was what he wanted.

Several years into our living together, Natasha fell in love, and I watched her do this same thing. I do not know if it bothered her, or if she even noticed it, but it seemed to me that she subtly became a different person around her boyfriend. One night in particular, I remember walking with them in the East Village when suddenly she was being twirled around on the sidewalk by him, like a little girl. I do not know if this actually happened (it seems extreme to me now) and, even if it did, my reaction may have had more to do with my fear of losing myself in love than with anything else, but I remember feeling physically sick at the sight of it. She seemed, I thought, completely out of touch with reality.

As Natasha became more involved in her relationship, our friendship began to disintegrate. It may have been due to a lot of things: I didn't particularly like her boyfriend, and I also probably didn't particularly like the fact that she had a boyfriend, as it brought up my own feelings of inadequacy with men. But I can also say that it wasn't just about Natasha, because similar scenarios were playing themselves out in all areas of my life. At the magazine, where I had once tried to develop friendships, I took myself out of the social loop. I was now simply focused on getting my work done without unnecessary distractions. In my other friendships, with acquaintances whom I might have spoken to once a week or so before, I gradually withdrew as well. It wasn't conscious; it just seemed to happen. I was busy, and I had to cancel once, and then I had to cancel again. Eventually, the calls tapered off. I still went out regularly at night, but I noticed that I no longer really engaged with the people I met at parties or clubs or readings. I simply didn't care what they had to say. I also began to realize that I didn't know what would make me happy anymore. Everything, even and perhaps particularly the good things, just seemed to contribute to the sinking feeling I had that I was missing my own life.

The other day I was in a bookstore, leafing through a play about a thirty-two-year-old woman who is a virgin. The playwright described her as having "hungry ears." I had never quite put my finger on it before, but that is exactly what it is like to be a virgin for a long time. It makes you feel almost psychotically energetic, with every pore of your being wanting to take something on. Standing there, reading this character's words, I remembered all of my old feelings of never really getting to anybody, never really making an impact. I saw that that was what so many discussions with my therapist had been about, when he would say something like how was your day, and I would say fine, and then I would admit only half-kiddingly that I'd actually felt like killing someone on the way in. Just to be done with it, I would tell him, just to exorcise myself of the incurable tension and sadness and frustration that I felt so basically but which I could never seem to do anything about.

At the time, I didn't know for sure but I had a few guesses as to why I felt this way. It was probably because I wasn't successful enough yet, or maybe because I really was smarter and stronger than everybody else. My therapist suggested that perhaps I was drinking too much coffee. Coffee had been known to increase anxiety in people, and maybe it had even played a part in my recent panic attacks, he said.

I can describe my panic attacks now—I had two, over the course of several months during my last year in New York—as the logical next step in the way my thought process was working in those days. I was thinking so much and was so tightly wound, both physically and mentally, that I am only surprised that I didn't have more of these attacks. The best way I can describe them is as a freezing of the mind. When they occurred, I could only move my eyes from one end of a room to the other with great effort, and holding a linear conversation became difficult.

Both of my panic attacks were triggered by contact with my

father. The first occurred while I was on the phone with him, sitting on the couch in my apartment. I was explaining that my boss had agreed to help me find a new job, when suddenly I couldn't seem to move my gaze from the window to the book-shelf. I described to my father what was happening. I told him that I felt like I was hypnotized or stoned, and I asked him if he thought I might be in shock that my boss was being so nice to me—that not being something I was used to from men. He said he didn't know, and neither did I, and then we quickly hung up. After briefly considering calling a hospital, I escaped my fear by lying down to sleep. The next and last time it hap-pened, I was leafing through my files at work when I came upon a fax that I'd sent several days earlier. It looked like I had signed my father's name to it instead of my own. Immediately, I was back in this strange zone.

I don't know why my father figured so prominently in these episodes. We had been going through a stressful time, but our problems were vague. I am not sure if it was before or after this, but at one point I refused to speak to him for an entire year while I was in New York. My decision had been sparked by an afternoon I spent with him during one of my Christmas vaca-tions in L.A., when he and I had been driving to a town about an hour away. He'd become upset because I had my period and I had forgotten to bring along extra protection. When I'd asked if we could go to a convenience store so I could run in and buy a few things, he'd begun attacking me for being thoughtless of "his afternoon" and for taking up too much time with my own needs. When we finally stopped, I went in to buy what I needed, and he placed a phone call to my mother to tell her what was happening. But her reaction—that it didn't sound like anything to get particularly upset about—only enraged him more. When we got back in the car, he decided that we should just go home, and he spent the next forty-five minutes or so shouting jibes, insults, and obscenities at me. We had been having big fights like this regularly, ever since I could remember, but sitting next to him that afternoon, squinting my eyes from the glare of the L.A. sun, I realized something. I realized that I had always felt that my father didn't like me. Even as a little girl, I had been sure that he favored my sister. I could never figure it out. I knew I was just as pretty, just as smart as she was, yet he still liked her more. I had decided finally that he must have seen some flaw in me that I couldn't detect. And that day in the car, I realized that that was what all of our fights had ultimately been about on my end: I was trying to prove to him that he was wrong about me. I decided I wasn't going to do it anymore.

I didn't speak to my father much for the rest of my vacation, and when I got back to New York, I told him that I needed some time. I wanted to establish an adult relationship with him, I said, because I wasn't a kid anymore.

The day I turned twenty-five, I decided to leave New York. I had been to a party the night before and felt the by now familiar sensation of walking around inside a glass box, not communicating with anyone but trying to act as if I were. When I told the friend I had come with that I was leaving the party, she had been momentarily concerned but then let me go, and as I began walking home, through SoHo on my way to the East Village, it dawned on me that I was the only one living my life, no one else was, and that I was the only one unhappy in it. I knew then that I couldn't keep pretending anymore. Everything that was supposed to make me happy was happening, and yet all I could feel was this increasing pain, coming from some place I couldn't identify. I'd spent most of the past year wondering why, blaming myself, thinking it was my fault. Now I was just tired. All I knew was that my life looked good on paper, but it didn't feel that way.

The next morning, I woke up in tears. I booked a plane to L.A. for the following day and went home for two weeks. Two weeks after that, I left New York for good. I didn't have a plan. I just went back to California to live with my parents for a while, and to rest. I had no idea what I was doing, but I also knew that I didn't really have a choice anymore. The only thing to do was to dive into the blackness.

When I slept with someone for the first time six months later, it was in a bedroom at a party in the Hollywood hills, with someone I'd met the week before. I'd been on a date when I'd been introduced to this man and had initially thought I didn't like him, but then I hadn't been able to get him out of my mind for the next several days. The next week, he had called to invite me to this party.

We were impossible as a serious proposition, I knew—he was married and I was leaving for a summer in London the following week—but I had a feeling we might sleep together. And when, that night, it had happened, I had suddenly felt as if the weight I'd been carrying around with me all of those years had just dissolved. I felt light. My first impulse was to gleefully but quietly crawl out of bed and speed home to call all of my friends, but I stayed. And as I lay there next to this stranger, I felt still for the first time in years.

I was in a daze during the next week, my last in L.A. I spent most nights with this man, drinking, talking, fooling around in dark bars or at his place, and I had the sensation that I was gliding through the hours. He purported to be upset that I hadn't told him beforehand that I was a virgin (although the fact itself put delight in his eyes); if he had known, he said in his outlandish way, we could have "made a thing of it," a thing involving champagne and sparklers and a big hotel bed. He made me laugh.

Everything, even the small, mundane things, seemed different in those first few days. Men who I saw on the street, bought things from, talked to on the phone—they all suddenly seemed like potential flings. I would find myself thinking: I could sleep with him. Sex seemed hyperreal, a constant option. I could do it, I knew what it was now, I was in on the secret. One afternoon, driving on the freeway alone, I remember trying to name what was happening to me, trying on words like "liaison" and "affair" in connection with myself.

On my last night with this man then, when I had to catch a plane in the morning and we were both going to sleep, I remember I started quietly crying next to him. When he asked me about it, I said I didn't know why but I just felt somehow sad about the whole thing, that this was all that there was. Maybe it did have to do with the fact that I was leaving, or that we weren't in love, but it was also more than that. It was a deeper feeling. At first he began apologizing a little, but then he said he knew what I meant. He was sad too, he said. Sex was sad to him because it's as close as you can get to someone, but it's also a limit, it's something that you cannot go beyond. I closed my eyes and kept listening.

ambition

I n my head, the sound of the career woman is the faint echo of high heels. It is the sound I hear now, when I think about Sarah and me, click-click-clicking down the street in our designer shoes all those years ago, walking block after block after block on indestructible urban pavement, from our fancy Madison Avenue offices to our downtown starter apartments, madly discussing our brilliant careers. Or what would become our brilliant careers. Or how we would build our brilliant careers. We were young and we were unstoppable—in our twenties, in publishing, in Manhattan. We were media girls. We had pointy shoes and sharp personalities.

I'd moved to New York when I'd first started at Barnard, a transfer student from a little college in Oregon, at twenty, and Sarah had moved there two years later, when she'd graduated from another Seven Sisters school. The story of how we met goes back to a little East Village place called Max Fish that I went to a lot in those days, and where girls and guys would go to pick each other out in methods not as sleazy, or simple, as pointing, but almost as raw and confused—although in completely different ways. It was very New York: The kind of place that seemed to exist so exactly for us, for the exact kind of girls we were, the slacker-at-a-high-level kind of place where the boys played in bands and did the weeknight shift at Kinko's, but where they all seemed like the type who might break out and become rock stars. After all, they were so fucking cute, and they'd made it to Manhattan already (a couple of the ones I met during this time, in fact, did). And then one night my friend Natasha met another boy there, Wes—he was a writer this time, I dimly recall, not a guitar player—and I became friends with him too. I'd go out on double dates with them sometimes, being paired with his friend Patrick, who straddled that fine line between being fucked-up enough to interest me but also too fucked-up to allow me to relax. (He was barely verbal, but he'd do things like, mid-date, ask me to leave the restaurant with him and get me high and ask me to hold his hand in a doorway. It freaked my twenty-one-year-old self out.) And then one night a couple of weeks into it, when Wes was unknowingly on the verge of becoming a distant memory to us all—he was psychopharmacologically medicated to the point that he'd fall asleep mid-makeout with Natasha, and it worried her—he ended up introducing me to Sarah, someone who would become many things to me, but for some reason now it seems most apt to describe her as my partner in crime, and I mean that in the best and worst way.

Sarah he knew only peripherally, he told me one night when I told him I was trying to break into magazines, but she had recently landed a job at *Harper's Bazaar*. *Harper's Bazaar* had just "relaunched," as they say in magazines, meaning that it had just undergone a radical makeover on every level—it had a new editor in chief, Brit Liz Tilberis, who had brought in an entirely new vision, and the vision was a radical departure from what *Bazaar* had become by then, which was a sort of uptown *Glamour*, and which appeared to be as much of an oxymoron as it sounds. But this new *Bazaar* had struck me with a visual electricity when I'd first seen it on the newsstand a couple of weeks before: It featured Linda Evangelista, her face, and her hand held above it, with her elegant and irreverent fingers catching the "falling" last "a" in *Bazaar*. ENTER THE ERA OF ELEGANCE, it read, and it stopped me dead in my Fifth Avenue tracks. It was the kind of thing I lived for, this moment, the moment when a magazine's immediacy—it is, after all, one of the only highly visual mediums that comes out every single month—shows you what you were thinking, or rather craving, but you didn't yet know. It is the moment when you glimpse *where you are going*. I couldn't believe this girl, Wes's friend, had a job there. "Do you want me to introduce you?" he asked.

Sarah came to the door of her Chelsea two-bedroom bouncing. Or so she seemed to be. She opened the door and she was small—only about five-foot-two, and adorable in the way that she seemed like something Walt Disney might have thought up but then misunderstood once she'd come alive and had a mind of her own. She had dark, dark brown hair and red, red lipstick on and white, white skin and a certain gravity to her. She was Snow White crossed with Betty Boop, if they'd gone shopping at Barneys. She welcomed me in.

It was a weeknight, around nine or so, and I had a manila folder with me. Into it, I'd thrown my resumé and a couple of clips of things I'd had published during college, things a series of internships had led me to. Among others, there was a piece about student activism that had appeared in *Lear's*, the first magazine aimed at women who "weren't born yesterday" (i.e., forty and over), and which was started by Frances Lear, Norman Lear's ex-wife. That piece had delighted my Oregon friends at the time, as much because they were pictured hanging on and off the letters of the headline as though it were a jungle gym as anything else. I also showed her my piece on Middle Eastern terrorism, which had been a paper for a poli sci class originally but which had then been published in a quasi-academic journal run by someone my father knew. In my contributor photo, Sarah and I decided that I either looked like an Armenian terrorist or a hip New Yorker. In some ways, then, neither one of us really knew the difference.

She seemed impressed—she'd never had anything of any real length published, she said—and told me she'd give it all to her boss, who would know if there were any openings at *Bazaar* in the next few months. I was very thankful, and we talked a little about her job. She was the fashion features assistant, so she wrote a lot of the fashion copy. She was the girl who wrote the headlines for stories on things like fur and diamonds and denim ("Fur Sure!," "Diamonds and Girls," "Good Jeans," she said nonchalantly as we flipped by her headlines in the current issue, echoing the words printed on the glossy pages) and who wrote the breezy text for fashion features, telling you and me what the models were wearing. I knew she hadn't written the cover line, ENTER THE ERA OF ELEGANCE (she hadn't been on staff at the magazine yet), but I also knew it was conceivable that she would write the next one like it.

Before I left that night, we made plans to hang out. We were supposed to go to Max Fish one evening in fact but nei-ther one of us called, in a display of either remarkable absent-mindedness, or an initial show of will—a grab from both ends at a power dynamic?—or a display of the young urban ennui ("Why even get out of bed tonight?" it's possible I wondered) that I sometimes felt in those early-twenties days. It was proba-bly a little bit of everything; in any case, I didn't worry about it. We made plans again, I'm pretty sure, a couple of weeks later. But I can't remember what we did, if anything.

Instead, the first thing that makes a really big impression on me regarding our friendship is a fight we had. At one point early on, Sarah lent me an extra futon she'd had lying around. Several months later then, I was moving so I had to get rid of it. I didn't know exactly what to do with the futon, though, so I called her and asked if she wanted it back. She did, but couldn't figure out how to transport it, so she'd said I might as well just put it out on the sidewalk, in the hopes that some homeless or otherwise needy and savvy person would come and get it and take it and enjoy it, like people always do in New York. That's my recollection of what happened. But Sarah felt that I hadn't given her enough lead time to retrieve the futon and she'd been forced to give it up. So she got mad. And the last thing I remember about it all is an uncomfortable phone call I had with her mother, who was visiting her around this time and who, I got the distinct impression, was mad at me by proxy. After that, Sarah and I didn't talk for about a year.

It was too soon to have a fight like this, I remember thinking, we didn't know each other well enough. It was like fighting with a guy about marriage when you've only been dating for about a month: There's nothing to hold the relationship up under the weight of such a thing. So our friendship just seemed to evaporate. We kept running into each other, occasionally and awkwardly passing each other on the street, as by that time we both worked at the same company: Condé Nast. She was now at *Mademoiselle*, in a job I'd ironically helped her to get after *Bazaar* had fallen through, and I was at *Condé Nast Traveler*, where I'd landed a position several months after meeting her. So we'd see each other on the street, and pass each other, perhaps occasionally in those heels I still sometimes fadingly hear. But in those moments we didn't say anything, we just kept on walking by, trying not to look in the way that it's easy to pretend you don't see someone in the flurry of midtown New York. But what we were really showing each other all those months, in those somewhat frequent moments, was hardness. We had met our match, but to make it clear we had to, for a solid year, completely miss each other. We had to create a vacuum as a sort of show of will. And so we did, inevitably, for a long long time.

And then one day she came up to me. It was on Madison,

and we hadn't spoken in forever, but she came right over to me, in the middle of the sidewalk, and we started talking and we were friends again. And after that we were close, maybe closer than we ever could have been if we'd had a regular beginning to it all.

It was, that lost year, good timing: It prepared me for our friendship in a way I couldn't have anticipated. In the meantime, as I've mentioned, I'd gotten a job at Condé Nast. Before that, though, I'd been working at *The Nation* up until graduation, for the second half of my senior year, and then I'd been temping, to make money, and interviewing for what seemed like an endless amount of time but was really only six months. I'd decided that I wanted to move up in the world after *The Nation*, knowing even then that I was moving up in a very particular way, in a superficial way, but I didn't care. I wanted to get out of the left-wing perpetual marginalization—courage and convictions be damned—that a political institution like *The Nation* provided, and into the plush glass-enclosed skyscraper that Condé Nast was. It had been a gradual shift in that direction over the course of the first summer I was out of school: I'd had an interview to work for the Armenian ambassador to the United Nations that I'd taken very seriously and wanted quite badly, and when I'd been offered an entrée to the Condé Nast human resources department, I'd initially had a snobby reaction, saying I didn't see myself working at a place like *Glamour*, though maybe perhaps *Vogue* or *Vanity Fair*. But I was taking every opportunity I got after a while, so I eventually asked the person who'd suggested Condé Nast—a family friend who was a contributing editor at several of the magazines—to pass my things along. And then, at some point—perhaps after I'd glided up to the HR department, and sat in the high-fashion-plate-filled lobby, and looked at the stone 350, as in 350 Madison (Condé Nast's flagship building), I'd decided that this was the place for me. I'd had a fine interview with the director of human resources then, but was sure I failed the typing test she gave me, and I began to think of her fearfully in later months as the gateway to a world I wanted to enter more than as a person.

In fact, I didn't get the first job I was up for at the company, an assistantship at *Vanity Fair*. By this time, though, several months into my job search, I was less heartbroken than simply sharply alarmed by this failure, the news of which I received in my temporary cubicle at Chase Manhattan Bank in Brooklyn. The day I found out happened to be my twenty-second birthday too, and I thought, in an unserious way, of suicide.

And then I had my second interview. It was at a magazine, *Traveler*, that I'd only had a chance to leaf through, having grabbed a copy at a newsstand hours before my interview. But I hoped I'd gathered enough information about it for the meeting to go well. I was ushered into my soon-to-be boss's office, an editor in chief's lair, in the corner, high up, big as a living room, with a marble-topped table in the middle and National Magazine Awards lining the shelves and semi-tinted windows that gave the whole place a sense of existing in a sort of softened reality. It was an effect that was echoed by my boss-to-be's demeanor. It was as though he, charming and

Harvard-educated and smoothly funny, was tinted with afflu-
ence himself. I wanted to be too.

I started talking. It was a story I'd been through enough
times by that point to feel that I was actually delivering a
monologue, one entertaining and personality-driven in parts
but also hopefully brief and informative enough to impart who
I was. It had, by that time, I thought, a certain style. I was in
command of the material: I grew up here, I did my thesis on
this, I held an internship there, I can be funny in this way. And
then he asked me several questions, the only one of which I
can remember is, did I know who Harry Evans was? The cor-
rect answer was, Harry was the founder of *Traveler* (as well as
the ex-editor of the London *Times*). But I liked my answer better: Sure, I said with a smile. He was Tina Brown's husband.

I knew that, and most of the other things I knew about New
York media, the same way I knew about Hollywood and movies
and celebrities, and I saw all of these things, I think appropri-
ately, as being pretty much the same thing. I knew about them
because I read, and looked at, the right things—even before I
entered the media world, I watched it. I perused, nearly religiously, *New York* magazine and *The New York Observer* and
The New York Times and *W.* And that was how, initially, I got
to know the people, the players, in the Manhattan game. It was
easy for me, and it was fun. And that's how I saw it, or pretended I did: as a game. I knew instinctually that, to play at all,
you had to. But I also knew you somehow had to see it as a real
game to take it seriously enough to join in. In a conversation
that made a huge impression on me, Tom, by then my boss,
would later allude to the key to life. "It's much simpler than

most people think," he told me. "It's a game, and there are rules. And if you can learn them, it's easy to win." I was delighted (it didn't occur to me he might be kidding), but I didn't want to press my luck: I didn't ask him what the rules were until months later. By that time, though, he didn't remember the conversation and said he had no idea what I was talking about. I was incredibly disappointed.

I'd been watching the game, or the winners, or this alternate world, the media world, since before I can remember. I'd been, in a way, born into this sort of observation. For I am the child of a child of famous people (my grandfather was an author, and my step-grandfather was a movie star), so I felt somehow a part of this universe—the Hollywood/New York fantasy nexus that is chronicled on paper and on TV—yet completely not a part of it from the time I was little. I didn't have a whole lot of contact with these famous relatives, but I had enough. And I had it in various ways. Sometimes, they would come to visit me and my family in our tiny community on the coast of California, being driven in their glossy black limo the hairpin-curve-filled hour through trees and dirt and nature until they finally reached us in their immaculate clothes, smelling enchantingly artificial to me, wearing Technicolor-smooth perfect things and bringing us gifts from another universe. One time, I remember, it was a set of Raggedy Ann and Andy dolls that were twice as big as we were: My siblings and I couldn't even play with them, the toys were so oversized. And unfortunately, although it almost seemed as if they were magical, they weren't alive. We wished they were. I wondered where they would have taken us.

On these visits, it was as though my relatives were as different from my exceedingly human self and my siblings, and my hippie-ish parents and our disarrayed house smack dab in the middle of a country meadow, as real life and a magazine layout. They seemed as though they'd been photographed by a different camera, as though they existed in a cleaner, more perfect place, like paper dolls set loose in real life—ours. They seemed like they'd stepped straight off the page, or climbed daintily out of the TV. Of course, to me, in a way they had. For my step-grandfather was not only a movie star, but my grandmother was even somewhat famous too, and so occasionally, probably in reality as often as or more often than I actually saw them, I saw them in these other mediums. When they didn't come to visit, I might catch them on TV attending the Academy Awards (that is, when we had a TV—which was only when my grandmother had sent another one along for Christmas and my mother had yet to throw it screamingly into the garbage can in front of our house, in a primal wail against mainstream culture and bullshit and materialism), or in a magazine layout, or in a movie when we went to the cinema.

The other way I'd see them, of course, was on the infrequent occasions when we'd go to visit them, which were equally surreal—particularly in the case of my grandmother and step-grandfather. We'd land in L.A., for some reason usually just my father and me solo, and the first thing I remember making an impression on me on these visits is the spinning planetlike restaurant right outside LAX, which to this day still resembles a UFO on stilts to me more than anything else. It was as though we were landing on another planet, and there was a spaceship: Spock, or my grandmother, might have been inside.

And then we'd visit them in their big pink house in spanking new–sounding Pacific Palisades, near a cliff that might as well have been the edge of the earth. (This pink house was so palatial that my little brother, upon seeing it for the first time, had asked in his kid voice from the backseat, "Is this the Holiday Inn?") And we'd eat whatever was served to us (alien food like hamburgers and Coke!), and my grandmother would give us things (bracelets; a pearl necklace once; another time an Elsa Peretti pen from Tiffany's when I must have been about nine), and we'd go to restaurants where she and my Uncle Walter (as I called my step-grandfather) would order food that wasn't even on the menu and if they got a phone call, the maître d' would bring the phone to the table. It was unbelievable and entertaining and desperation-inducing in me, somehow.

And then we'd go home. And I wouldn't exactly be upset, so much—I liked my life, and I loved my family and my friends, and I was good at school, and I was happy—but on some level everything would be wrong after that. It would look wrong. I had mildew behind my bed, and I'd try to hide it, and the house would be messy when I'd get home from school, and I'd yell. I don't even know that I wanted to live in the pink house in particular, but I know that I did want to live in the closest thing to it in my little town: The lone house with a lawn—a regular, green, perfect mowed lawn—and a white picket fence around it that looked like it had been built yesterday. But I would never live there as a kid. I would always live in the other house, and I would always fly home from L.A. I might as well have been flying back from Narnia. For all of this—all of this contact with these relatives—was like going to Disneyland. But it was real. Or at least I was pretty sure it was, but I never got to hang out long enough to figure it all out.

I did think I had a knack for it, though, for blending in in this other world. Maybe my secret was just that I didn't want to let on how amazing, truly amazing, it all was to me, so I didn't. I kept a grip. And the way I remember that I demonstrated this grip was when, beautifully apt as it seems to me now, my grandmother would take us shopping. My sister and my mother would go wild on these sprees—buying unearthly amounts of things, like lottery winners given just a few hours to purchase all that they'd dreamed of, my baby sister coming home from one such day, I remember, with dozens of fairy-princess dresses in all shades of pastel, with puffy sleeves and puffed-out skirts and all manner of gauze and silk and ruffles thrown in for pretty measure and, on another day, my fashion-loving but usually self-sacrificing mother buying a series of outfits the likes of which I'd never seen before. But not me. I—after Grandma Carol and I had valeted at the top-notch department store that she took me to in the Rolls she drove so recklessly as to seem invincible, and after I'd watched her splash on all manner of perfume at the cosmetics counter as liberally as she might water—would choose a few simple classic pieces that I'd actually wear. I knew what I wanted, and I wanted what I got. I didn't lose my head; I chose carefully and well. And when we returned at night to the house, my grandmother would tell everyone this: "She knows how to shop."

So I was included in the unrealness of it all, and I wasn't. I was allowed to occasionally step into the fantasy and then I was promptly expelled. It wasn't my life, but it was a small postcard in my book. It was an escape hatch, a secret (trap?) door, a world I could only occasionally visit. But it could, conceivably, when I grew up, be mine: *I knew how to shop.* The rest of the time, I read about it. In *W, People, Vogue,* places like that. I suppose it is inevitable that I moved to New York at twenty and went promptly to work for the dream machine of magazines.

I got the job at *Traveler.* It was January of 1993, and at first it was exciting. I made do with no real clothes and no trust fund (a rarity, I soon realized, at that company, where Prada bags reigned and Calvin-everything permeated the very air, turning it into a sort of capitalistic perfume), and I kept quiet and made coffee and started writing and editing. I prided myself on doing my job perfectly and, I believe, in perhaps the only instance in my life that I would claim this, that I did. I concentrated and I watched, like I'd watched television or read magazines as a child and then teenager. And I did all of this with nervousness and sometimes even fear. I didn't want to be expelled. But when it became clear that I wouldn't be expelled—after a year or so, it must have been—although I still liked and respected my boss and coworkers, I no longer thought Condé Nast was all it was cracked up to be, and it occurs to me now that those two realizations were somehow related: If I wasn't going to be expelled, how *could* it be all that it was cracked up to be? But at the time, my feelings just read to me as the faintest inklings of boredom. And that was when Sarah and I started talking again.

Over the course of that next year, we became friends, casually. Our realities did not wholly overlap, our ambition did not become one and the same, one's intensified by the other's, until later. At first we simply started going to parties together. We started out by just having a lot of what we were told was, and what we at first wide-eyedly believed to be, fun. I needed a friend, that's all. Natasha, not only my apartment-mate but also my best friend up until then, had just become involved in her first serious relationship, so she was often gone. And she and I had less and less in common in other ways: She'd decided to become an actress, and her world had become one of auditions and other actors and agents and day jobs. Now, it also included a boyfriend, a lawyer who was nearly ten years her senior and who had a nicely sprawling apartment but, it seemed to me, the most boring *life* I could imagine. The corporate world? I'd barely even heard of it, I thought to myself, and I didn't care to now.

Mine, my life, and Sarah's too by then, was on the other hand hurtling toward a reality so many people had hurtled themselves toward before: Media Land. It is something that comes along with landing jobs like ours, Sarah's and mine, every year to unsuspecting but delighted twenty-one- and twenty-two-year-olds: You don't just get a job when you ride up the elevator for your first day at work in your glamour industry of choice, you get a life. You are passed along invitations from the senior people around (and also, in my case, hand-me-down dresses from *Vogue* editor Anna Wintour, via her good friend, *Traveler*'s literary editor) who are already overflowing with things to do and people to see. And soon enough, you yourself are targeted by the best and the brightest in every industry, who want coverage and know you're the window through which to get it. For even a little mention in a magazine like *Traveler* (which, like nearly all the Condé Nast rest, has a million readers a month) could change people's lives, and it did. So, in the hopes of that, I was, and Sarah was too, wooed and invited places and given things incessantly. And we didn't even really have to give anything back because there was always the promise that one day, we might. And that, apparently, was enough. We were on the *right* part of the food chain.

So we entered this land. It was a land of harshly beautiful women I wanted to be like, single nearly all, where movie screening passes and your name on the list at gallery openings and book parties in huge white seemingly-floating lofts were handed out like candy, and where incessantly chic quasi- and sometimes not so quasi-famous people lived. It was a fast world, too—due to the three-month lead time magazines need, most everything you went to was occurring three months before it would for the rest of the world, any product launch or fashion show or movie peek. So you were living, almost literally, in a sort of never-never land, a time warp of the future, brought to you especially. You were surfing the edge of the curve before anyone else: You were there.

I think, still, that magazines—especially fashion magazines—are the place where glamour is created, even more than in Hollywood or in any other form of media, in a way. And so this was the world created by the glamour-creators for themselves.

To me, at first, it looked a lot like that world my grandparents had given me a glimpse into, although it was new and improved and much more sophisticated. I was older now, and ready. It was like a game again, though, and I was in some ways like a kid playing Candy Land.

So Sarah and I passed Go. We had our passes—as I've said, our low-level jobs at high-level companies—and we entered and went on what sometimes felt like a mad spree. The parties and events varied. I was, soon enough, handling most of the beauty world for *Traveler*, which meant I wrote and edited its monthly beauty page. It was a small part of my magazine, but a big part of others, and there was an entire publicity machine which had sprung up around it. I could have, as many a young girl editor at Condé Nast did, spent much of my work time at functions relating to it: Launches of brand-new products every brand-new season took the form of everything from early morning formal breakfasts high up in the penthouses of topflight hotels (Chanel's new cellulite cream, which was explained with graphs and visuals so graphic you didn't want to eat the scones or drink the tea anymore, after a while) to trips (the recently renovated Golden Door spa) to parties (Elizabeth Hurley being introduced as the new face of Lauder). Most of these were boring to me after the initial oddity wore off, but there are ones that I still remember indelibly because of their sheer indulgence. Elizabeth Arden was introducing its perfume "True Love," for example, and we were all taken to the ballroom of the Stanhope for a many-coursed "wedding" lunch with a model "bride" wafting in and out, and then to its interminably vast penthouse for the "reception." There, editors put their heads through cutouts that "dressed" them as brides and their pictures were snapped by Bill Cunningham, the photographer famous in these circles for taking the impromptu photographs of women on Manhattan streets that run in the Sunday *Times*'s "On the Street" fashion column. Once, Cunningham had snapped my picture, on Madison, and it was one of the surest signs yet, I remember thinking, that I'd arrived.

The stream of such beauty events was endless, but I chose to stem the tide and focus on other things, of which there were many after a while, and which you knew of through people you met at the best of these things and who hooked you into a better scene. Of course, many others were just a part of the natural banquet of New York. Sarah and I went to it all. We went to the launch party for our new rock star friends' CD—no, they weren't yet superfamous, but they were in heavy rotation on MTV; we went to the opening of Karl Lagerfeld's "serious" photography exhibit downtown, dodging the PETA protestors as we walked in behind Anna Wintour and squinting at the lights, camera, and action that attended Claudia Schiffer's passing by; we went to the MTV Video Music Awards' on-air after-party, fighting our way through the NYPD barricades to let them know that we were the people who were supposed to be let in and, in the days afterward, we watched it all later on television.

This last event, now, strikes me as the most insane and also interesting of the bunch, because we were, at that party, inside the TV—in those moments we had broken through its glass. It is the kind of moment that I now see as being quintessentially New York, and certainly a lethal ingredient in the cocktail of that city that I know others drink gladly as well. Years later, after JFK, Jr., had just died, I would run into an old sometime-boyfriend who still lived in New York, and he would describe drowning his sorrows in a beer at a bar in his TriBeCa neighborhood where Kennedy had also lived, and watching TV coverage of the event from this establishment, and seeing that the coverage was in fact of the bar itself. He was looking to the TV to find news of the tragedy, yet it just reflected himself back to him. It was, he said, "weird." Like I had been all those years ago, he was, at that moment, inside the black box. And even though it had been so long ago for me, my similar moments in New York had made a big impression. I would envision them again, more literally, years later in L.A., when I wrote a poem about climbing into the television itself. In the poem, I was wearing those high heels again, and on the way in I bloodied my ankles but I didn't care.

Another party moment that stands out to me is the first time I saw Tina Brown, the woman who at that point was my role model. In a rare moment of ticket-buying, Sarah and I were among the youngest to attend a "discussion" on celebrity at the Public Theater, an event which was inspired by and designed to publicize the new Clive James series and corresponding television show on the topic. The panel was, again, the ubiquitous Wintour (who stayed bespectacled, à la Jackie O, the whole time); a couple of literary men (Norman Mailer, perhaps, among them; I can't quite remember); no doubt a Billy Norwich type (he was then the society columnist for *The Observer*), if not he himself; Fran Lebowitz; and, of course, a significant part of the reason we were attending this event and the woman who had transformed this ticket into a hot one, Tina Brown. The discussion itself was disappointing—not half as good as the intricate and heated discussions Sarah and I would have on street corners at the point where our paths home diverged, having walked downtown from work, when we'd try to figure it out, celebrity: its allure, what it must be like, what its prevalence and importance meant about society, why some people we knew were obsessed with it and others were getting a taste of it. We were the experts, the truly possessed by this topic, and we might as well have been up there. We, after all, spent hours on that corner, somehow almost banging down the door to understanding.

Afterward, there was a reception in the lobby and Tina was there. We fluttered around her, in the same room but too shy to say anything. In some way, it was as though we weren't there, but we were. And after a while, the intense excitement we took in this (the crashers were in the castle!) wore off, and we began to feel oddly outside the room.

The Tina event was probably the most understandable—if among the most dramatic—example of when we felt, and in fact were, somewhat invisible, but it was also a familiar feeling after a while to both Sarah and me. We would have the same feeling, although we couldn't articulate it to each other then, when we'd go to New York's trendiest bars, dark beautiful places where celebrities appeared at every turn—Kate Moss was waiting to use the bathroom, the guy who'd caught your eye in the corner turned out to be Johnny Depp, etc. It wasn't as though we had no overlap with this world—one of Sarah's best friends had started dating a well-known fashion designer, and we'd all hang out; we'd go to parties sometimes with budding rock stars; and to book launches for friends of ours who had, as of late, been transformed into the young literati—but we still felt overridingly invisible, as though we could see them but they couldn't see us. We were ghosts, and after a while we knew it.

We were also becoming ghosts because of how fully we subscribed to the values of celebrity, and how eager we had been not only to jump into the swath of glitter that the media professional's life and its attending elements brought along with it, but to live by this glitter, as though simply chasing it meant more even than actually catching anything else. I was a ghost, and I knew I was one night when, walking home, I thought to myself that the only two things I believed in anymore were beauty and power. But even this thought, which did alarm me somewhat, I knew deep down did so more because I had less of these things than I wanted than because of the belief itself.

But although I was beginning to feel something was wrong, at that point it simply read to me as the same kind of wrong I'd felt as a child, when I'd return from Hollywood and a visit with my grandmother. My world was wrong, and the way to right it was to enter the other one. What this need translated into, now that I was an adult, was ambition. My ambition was, in some naked sense, to do well career-wise, but it was also to transcend, to fall, like Alice, into a whole other dimension. To not only ascend as a media professional, but to join the world on the page, to not only cover it and look at it, but to engage in it and ultimately *be* in it. I wanted my life to be a magazine layout, a television show, a movie. And the only way I knew how to try to succeed in this capacity was to work harder and harder, and to direct it all at that other world in the best way I knew how.

So every morning I would get up, stumble out of bed around eight, and into the bathroom—where I remember on more than one occasion trembling with fear until I fully woke up (fear of what, I never knew; it was just sheer terror)—and brush my teeth, wash my face, get dressed, and walk to work. I didn't usually wear high heels in fact—no, that was only in my mind's eye—but I did walk those forty or so blocks each way, every day. And when I arrived at the office, I would have a butterless plain bagel and a large coffee, and I would take a certain amount of hard joy in sitting down at my desk, with my computer and my phone and my in-box and my adjustable chair, and having the world, increasingly and with every passing day—or so it seemed for a while—at my fingertips. I liked the idea of it.

My job at *Traveler,* soon, wasn't enough for me, though, and although I gradually began doing more creative things—writing front-of-book pieces, editing various columns—I also needed something more to keep me engaged. So I started doing freelance work, writing. I got my first assignment from *Premiere,* to interview the filmmaker Atom Egoyan, and I sped up to a coffee shop near Lincoln Center one afternoon during lunch with my tape recorder for my first real celebrity interview. I'd prepared by watching everything he had done—only about five or six films, but all with the depth of good literature—and we had a great interview about metaphor, media, immigration, and art. Condensing it down to a hundred and fifty words was not easy and, in fact, impossible if I wanted to preserve any real essence of our exchange. But I spent the next two weeks trying—obsessively and strivingly, but under the guise of simply "pacing" myself—and I ended up creating, instead, a little candy of a piece that was snappy and clever. If it wasn't what it might have been, I also knew that this first freelance piece of mine had its own certain quality. And I discovered I was good at giving things this quality. I was, as one of my friends at *Traveler* used to tell me, simply a natural at achieving the "media voice."

Premiere liked the piece, and ran it at the bottom of a page with a small picture. The magazine was beamed to every supermarket and bookstore in America, I happily thought to myself sometimes that month, and it had my name in it. Christian Slater was on the cover. I bought a couple of copies.

One thing that came out of it was that I got a call from an editor at *Interview* who had rejected the Egoyan idea (I'd offered it to him before taking it to *Premiere*) but obviously liked what I'd done with it elsewhere—and perhaps even more than that, I think now, liked the fact that I *had* done it elsewhere. He invited me to come down to his office to retrieve an assignment. This was not standard practice—usually, one would just get the specifics of something like this over the phone—but it was a nice gesture, a sort of get-to-know-you approach that I hoped would bode well for the future.

I walked into *Interview*'s SoHo lobby, with its Jeff Koons vacuum cleaners in airless glass containers stacked one on top of the other, and took the elevator up. The editor came out to greet me. He took me into his office, a small place with a window overlooking the city, and asked me what I wanted to do. I told him that I wanted to, ultimately, edit a magazine. He said I was a good writer. I smiled at his contradiction; flattering though it was, it also seemed he was trying to provoke me. He was in his late thirties, and his eyes lingered on me too long. We chatted for a while, and then he gave me the assignment— this one a hundred-worder—to cover a new movie that had been directed by Michael Apted. Then he took me into the private gallery that is adjacent to the magazine's offices, and showed me the Warhols that "Andy," Interview's founder, had bequeathed to them.

It was the beginning of what became a very odd interaction between the two of us, during which, over the course of several assignments, this editor ripped my writing to shreds and I responded in furious attempts to do better. We must have gone through five incarnations of that first piece, arguing over every single word, barring "the" and "and." At one point, several versions into it, he asked me if I wanted to start over. It was a betrayal, I felt. A couple of times I went down to his office again and we worked on the piece together, trying to hammer out one hundred perfect words with a kind of precision and tension that I had never experienced before. I didn't know then that this kind of thing leads to bad writing—at the time, it felt exhilarating. And at the same time, this editor also began doing a similar thing to me personally: asking me out, and not following up—not calling or standing me up. We did end up going to lunch a couple of times, though, during the first of which he kept nervously spilling water on himself and pointing

out celebrities: Did I see Mariel Hemingway behind us? I remember him asking me. It went on for weeks. I was angry, but
also amused and more interested than I wanted to admit. Because this editor, in some way I did not understand, was hitting
a nerve. He was giving me something to do. I needed it—
craved it—and I was grateful.

At some point then, a job came up at *Interview* for an associate editor, and this man suggested I apply for it. "Associate
editor: Me, at twenty-four!" I thought excitedly. It would be a
good title, a good job. But there was a hoop to jump through.
Before I could interview, this man asked me to come up with
several dozen feature ideas by that Friday, only three days away.
It was a tall order that I tried to, and did, fulfill on one level.
But on another level I remember being upset with myself because I didn't fulfill it as well as I thought I should have. I felt,
as I was brainstorming madly on those days and nights, that I
should have somehow been working more madly, not sleeping
at all, maybe taking drugs to do it. I felt that I was holding myself back from letting loose and doing the task with fury. I was
holding back somehow, I felt, from my own ambition. What
wouldn't let me break through?

And at the same time that I knew I felt this, I didn't know
exactly what I was looking for. Was it that I wanted the job?
Yes, but it was more than that. I was also looking for something
to happen, something to change. I was looking for that transcendence through professionalism, through ambition itself, to
work so hard that I'd be somehow flying through a sea of papers
and words and fast-moving chaos until I crashed on through to
the other side. What side, I'm not exactly sure, perhaps a side

that broke through the sound barrier into a sort of floating slo-
mo reality where I was weightless and everything was drifting
but less manically. It would be a fantasy, a new real. Where
everything was quiet. But I never did break through. And I
knew I never did, and I remember very palpably that I was mad
at myself about it.

One day not long after, Sarah called me up and told me that
she thought we should start a magazine of our own. She'd
thought about it, she said, for a while: She wanted it to be for
girls like us, and she wanted to call it *Sugar*. We talked, and I
mulled it over for a day or two, but I called her back and said
no. I told her that my parents had both been, and still were,
struggling freelance artists, so I knew the pitfalls of being
overly idealistic and of jumping in headfirst. I thought we
needed to know more. The idea of being able to do it in any
real way—not as just another 'zine—was too pie-in-the-sky, I
thought. I wanted to learn. And anyway, I said, who were we,
yet?

And then I spent the next several weeks being interviewed
around town. Even if I wasn't ready to start my own magazine,
I was ready to take the next step up professionally, and I met
with people both at *Interview* and at other magazines. I'd decided that next I wanted to work somewhere that was smaller
and newer, where I could have more responsibility, and I'd
written to several young editors who had just launched their
own magazines and set up meetings with them. Among them
was David Lauren, Ralph's son, who had just launched *Swing*,
an incarnation of an on-campus magazine he'd started in col-

lege, and which was now newly fortified with multispread layouts of advertising from his father and a distribution deal with
Hearst. I was ushered into his office immediately and then sat
there while he spoke on the phone for fifteen minutes, only
getting off long enough to tell me that he saw *Swing* as being a
sort of *U.S. News & World Report* for twentysomethings and
that he was very busy, and that I should come up with a couple
of ideas. When he hung up again for a moment, I told him
about an idea I had for a first-person column about the preju-
dice experienced by naturally skinny girls—a sort of reverse
snobbery—that I thought could make for a funny piece. I told
him that it would speak for those of us who gleefully identified with Kate Moss in the wake of the seemingly intermin-
able vogue of glamazon models like Cindy Crawford and Elle
Macpherson. He said great, and asked me to pitch it in writing.
I said I would, but as soon as I walked out onto Fifth Avenue, I
knew that I wouldn't. I just didn't feel like it. I wasn't that
interested.

I also met with a girl about my age who was the editor of a
new magazine that billed itself as covering Manhattan's high
life. When this girl came out to greet me, emerging from her
corner office in a huge loft space that was studded with hipper-
than-thou modern art and that housed editorial, she struck me
as being a beautiful doll. We walked into her office, and she
started talking. She told me that she had come in to New York
from the Hamptons, where she'd edited a sort of *W* for the
Long Island set (but wasn't *W* itself for the Long Island set? I
silently wondered). And then I started watching her. I'd heard
she was dating James Truman, the editorial director of Condé

Nast and the lust object of nearly every assistant—including me—at the company. And as I sat there, across from this young woman and her Bruce Naumans, which were hanging solidly, like endorsements, above her head, I kept watching her, and I realized she was flawless. We kept the meet and greet going for about a half hour and I left with an overwhelming feeling of aspiration. She appealed to my most basic Wasp envy. She was a girl who belonged in a sitting room gazing at expensive art, I thought as I walked home, while the cook made complicated things. She belonged in a grand apartment on the Upper East Side, dining amid crystal and candles, living the perfect life so all the rest of us could be assured that it still existed. She didn't strike me as knowing very much about magazines, that had been clear even in my daze—perhaps in fact responsible for it—but the meeting from the beginning hadn't been about that. I didn't want to work for her. I wanted to be her.

My reaction to this girl, while it may sound odd in the context of my ambition, was actually of a piece with it. For my ambition by that time was not just professional, it was ambition about life, about being the right kind of person, about looking the right way and talking the right way. It was the same species of ambition, in fact—though I could barely recognize it, let alone admit it out loud—that had contributed to my wanting the job at *Interview*, which I ultimately didn't get, but which I'd largely wanted in the first place because it would have given me ample time to flirt with the editor I had met there and to perhaps thereby become one half of something larger than ourselves—a couple living a particular sort of life. And mine was a shape of ambition that was well-suited to this profession—

the media life—where your after-hours are as important as your office hours, where lunch is the real event of the day, and where the evening's "press" events are as much a personal playground as a professional one. It is a structure, this blurring of the personal and the professional, that is necessary to do the particular kind of New York job that I aspired to do, and at first it appears to be blessedly work-free—and in a way, it is. But the flip side of it, of course, is that if you begin to care too much about your life—and try to shape it into some Platonic ideal of what it could be—and you can't relax, then it becomes the opposite. Your whole life is no longer personal, your whole life is professional. Building your life becomes your job, becomes your profession, and the main values that dictate what kind of life you want—or the kind of life I wanted—are somehow public. For they are based on a version of perfection outlined by outside sources, superficial sources, whose main criterion is what your life looks like. So you begin living a public life, a life whose values are defined by other people, by media people, by, finally, media itself, even though you aren't famous. No, you aren't famous, but you are living for your public anyway. And the result is that any personal life you may have had disappears. So I looked up to that girl who was dating James and editing that new magazine about New York. But I didn't want to work for her. As I said, she seemed to me to know little about magazines, and I had the same feeling about Lauren, yet they were striking out on their own. I called Sarah back. I told her yes.

We had our first *Sugar* magazine meeting on a Tuesday night. We began brainstorming. It was magic. Our job was to merge our world with a media project: We could create a fantasy on the page that reflected our reality a little more closely. *Sugar* would be a young women's magazine, and our focus would be on what was then called "alternative" culture, which included everything from independent film (just then hitting it big) to grunge rock (on the way out, but having changed the landscape seemingly permanently). We would cover all of it from the female point of view, meaning that we would talk about things the way girls talk about things. We would be the Liz Phair of magazines: honest, original, and graphic—culturally and emotionally so. That was our idea.

The notion of focusing on the cultural, in particular, had grown out of an insight I'd had one day in the New York Public Library. Sarah and I had started making after-work pilgrimages to the branch on Forty-second Street to fortify our arsenal creatively—looking at old issues of women's and girls' magazines, checking out books and articles about the eighteen-to-twenty-nine-year-old female demographic, reading up on its—or our—buying power. And so one day in the main reading room I found myself flipping through the latest issues of *Details* and *Mademoiselle* magazines. Sarah and I had long ago stopped even glancing through *Mademoiselle* but we both, at that point, read *Details* religiously. It was ironic—*Millie*, as it was called, was the magazine that the company we worked for aimed at us, yet we found it uninteresting to the point of being totally irrelevant. But *Details*, which was aimed at the men in our age group—and the gay ones in particular—was something we read. But I'd never understood why quite as clearly as I finally did that day in the library. As I flipped through *Millie*, through page after page of relationship quizzes and boy tips and fashion and beauty tidbits, it hit me that all of its editorial was directed inward: It was all about what was going on in my head—in the mythical "girl's" head. It was all about what she might be able to change, how she could be prettier, skinnier, and think about things more to make herself—myself—more attractive and receptive. It was reactive, it struck me then; it took place within the confines of girls' inner lives and was designed to direct our energy almost solely toward reinventing ourselves in the image of the "fantasy girl" who was featured on the fashion pages in every issue. This was as opposed to *Details* then, which, as I flipped through its pages that day in the library, I suddenly realized was all about things in the *outside* world—music, film, books—and people having lives, real actual out-in-the-world lives. In *Details*, there were "stunt" pieces about guys taking up race car driving, and first-person pieces about guys snooping in their girlfriends' medicine cabinets. And so it had hit me: Let's do a women's magazine about girls having real, outer lives in the world. Let's do something different: Let's stop chasing the fantasy.

We started meeting every Tuesday night in Sarah's apartment on Broadway and Twenty-first Street. We'd asked Sarah's friend Fred, an art assistant at a top fashion magazine, to be our art director; he agreed, completing the founding team. Sarah bought a how-to book on starting a magazine, and we began refining our point of view—our "editorial DNA," as Tina Brown calls it—and ultimately creating a prototype that realized our vision. We would, we decided, do a few things that were different than other magazines at that time. Sarah came up with the idea that we wouldn't use models but instead "real" girls in our fashion stories, and on our covers we wouldn't have models either—we would feature celebrities. (Calvin Klein hadn't yet done the former, and *Jane* magazine hadn't done the latter: Both were new ideas but, as we felt, just below the surface.) Another thing we decided we'd do differently was beauty, which we vowed only to cover in a light, almost humorous way. We would never do a feature on "how to wash your face," as we took to explaining it: That's how we described every stupid, beneath-us beauty feature we'd ever read. We would only do beauty stuff on cool, pretty things that encouraged creativity. We also had more and more specific visions as the days went on: One day, Sarah told me about an idea she had for a Courtney Love shoot that would feature the rocker dressed up as an angel with wings (when *Vanity Fair* did this six months later, we wondered if someone had heard our murmurings, but glumly decided it was just the collective unconscious; we wanted to hit the stands!).

So we met on Tuesdays, and we kept gradually gathering things—contacts, products, ideas—for our prototype. In the beginning, it was like putting material together for a collage that we would then arrange. I was in charge of creating the beauty and books sections, and so began surreptitiously, from my desk at Condé Nast, ordering in products to photograph: calling up London to order a new line of Mary Quant punkish nail polishes (pre–Hard Candy) that I'd read about in *New York*, having the latest books from Haitian writer Edwidge Danticat and the art world's Guerrilla Girls sent over. As I have said, Sarah and I also went to the library to do research and, I remember, one day we came upon an essay by Mary McCarthy critiquing women's magazines called "Up the Ladder from *Charm* to *Vogue*," and devoured it with delight: Someone else had thought about this stuff, and verbalized it! And Fred began creating visuals. We would sneak into his magazine's offices on weekends, and tiptoedly check out the untouched-up contact sheets of Cindy Crawford's cover shoot for its next issue while Fred pulled up designs he was thinking about for us. He also began contacting photographers, because we were going to need to do a fashion shoot. We started thinking about contributing editors too. Sarah enlisted a friend who was an MTV producer to be one; from a mutual friend, I got Elizabeth Wurtzel's number. She also loved the idea, and agreed to do it.

We were hit with a couple of challenges early on, but we rallied: A friend came back from a trip to London and told us he'd seen a magazine called *Sugar*, so we changed the name to *Bleach*. *Bleach* meant a lot of things. It was a reference (and tribute, of a sort) to Nirvana's first album, and Kurt Cobain had just died; it was a reference to every woman who'd cleaned her house with bleach while her husband was at work in the fifties, keeping everything clean and good and happy and normal in her family; it was a reference to the "white-out whitewash," as I described it, that every other women's magazine was when it came to acknowledging the truth of what it meant to be us; it was a reference to all the East Village girls, including me, who'd started bleaching chunks of their hair blond but leaving self-consciously undone parts, taking the notion of roots one step further, and thus screwing with the blond female ideal. The idea being: Fuck the fantasy. We decided that would be one of our tag lines. We'd put it on stickers, and hand them out late at night at clubs. Yeah: Fuck the fantasy. It felt good to say it, and it made us laugh, like gleefully wicked black-clad New York girls.

We were inspired. One night at a bar I remember Sarah telling me she thought she knew what Cobain must have felt like before Nirvana broke: Our *Bleach*, she felt, was riding the crest of that same kind of a wave. Women's magazines were ready to change. And we were passionate about it, about having an impact on, affecting the very thing we were transfixed by, the world on the page. And we *were* transfixed: Sometimes, she and Fred and I would sit around in her apartment silently, all three of us reading magazines for what now seems like hours. Now I believe we were looking for those moments, those electric moments like the one I'd experienced when I'd seen the new *Bazaar*, and we were looking for clues to how to create our own. I remember the three of us daydreaming about the future sometimes too: When *Bleach* came out and caught on, as we knew it would, we'd have the best tickets to all the "shows," next to people like Anna and Tina and Liz. And what would we do when James Truman called? I asked one night giddily. "James, I'm sorry, can you hold?" I pretended I would say. I'd tell him I was so busy, I told my co-editors then, I'd have to call him back. Of course, James would try to buy us, I went on, and of course we'd put him off—"but only after leading him on enough that he named a price!" I added joyfully. From that little one-bedroom on Twenty-first Street, we plotted our path. We would own New York.

It was a tradition we felt we belonged to, and Madonna was

on the deepest level our sister in crime. I had actually proposed at one point that *Bleach*'s tag line be, "A Post-Madonna Magazine for Women" ("fuck postmodern," I said to Sarah as I tried to sell her on it) and, in times of crisis, we would, as I had been doing since I was fifteen and proposed to Sarah that she start doing too, simply ask ourselves, "What would Madonna do?" That was what we invoked when our first truly big professional trial came up—our greatest pain but somehow glory at once: Fred wasn't working out. His designs, the ones he had shown us in his magazine's offices and which he'd been almost hyperactively enthusiastic about himself, leaving what we felt to be little room for criticism, simply didn't match our vision. It was an awkward situation—he was one of Sarah's best friends—but we knew what we had to do. The project was more important than each part of it; the professional had to be extricated from the personal. Madonna would fire him.

We called him up. It was a problem that had been brewing for weeks, but neither one of us was aware of how aware Fred was of it until we got him on the phone that day. When Sarah told him that we all had to talk and that he should come up to her apartment, he began screaming that he was sick of working with us and that he was sick of the power games and everything else, and, in a rage, on the phone, right there, he quit. Sarah hung up stunned at the meltdown she had just witnessed. But on some level, we both felt exhilarated. We were in the thick of a professional emergency: We were paying our dues, going through the rough spots, experiencing the rough and tumble reality of getting our hands dirty, taking the hits. We were handling something, because we had, finally, something to handle.

A month or so later, we read about Lawrence Temple in *Wired*. He was dubbed "the Sid Vicious of font design" (in a double profile of him and "the Beethoven" of the field), and we thought he might be our man, our post-Fred art director. That's what we needed: a visual Sid Vicious. We went to see him in his office downtown, and he seemed, on first impression, less like Sid and more like Big Bird. He was tall and lanky and eccentric. His aesthetic was Sid-like in its irreverence, though, and he told us that day that he was working on Japanese video games and commercials to make money. We liked him, and began telling him about our idea. We spoke feverishly: We told him about our world, our world on the page, trying to sell it to him. And we were also, in our fervor, somehow selling him ourselves, our passion and desperation to create this alternate version of reality that reflected us more clearly than media ever had, and that also responded to and acknowledged us. We needed, it felt in moments like this, to create it.

We described some of our ideas. We wanted to do new things in magazines, we told Lawrence, to be self-referential and make our notions about media itself come alive visually. I told him I thought it would be cool to do a shoot where all the girls were photographed interacting with media: reading *Vogue*, walking past a bigger-than-life-size billboard, watching *Baywatch*. Sarah had an idea for a cover too: She wanted to break the fourth wall, and have it look like the cover was coming out of the cover, as though the girl on the page was tearing through the page itself, bursting off the paper to come and get you.

We also offered him a third of the company. And as we did all of this, we pushed hard, we pushed hard in our first meeting as a high-powered team. After all, it was the first time we'd taken ourselves "public," so to speak, proclaiming ourselves self-created editrixes in a deadpan and real way on a professional cold call. We'd walked into this meeting as who we were going to be, not who we were. And we were self-convinced. "We're interested in giving you the opportunity to realize a full vision here, to create an aesthetic," we said. "There's nothing out there right now for *us*. Where does Courtney Love fit in in the culture? In women's media culture?" we asked. We told him we wanted to be that place. And we were sincere and hard driving. But he seemed on the fence. In fact, he'd seemed to be acting a little superior.

As we hit Broadway, we were flabbergasted. How could he not bite? But it didn't seem that he would, so we tried to redirect. "You know, Straws, I think we need a woman. Wouldn't it be great to get a woman?" Sarah said as we walked. We began talking about *Paper* magazine's art director then, a woman named Bridget, and how her eye combined the streamlined with the unmistakably female: She had subtly superimposed bubblelike circles all over a recent article we'd read, and it worked. In a fashion shoot we both remembered and which she'd overseen as well, she'd featured East Village–y looking models dressed in their own clothes and standing next to mismatched men, looking wittily like mail-order brides, we agreed. So we thought about approaching this woman, Bridget, drowning out our disappointment with our ever-ready supply of more drive. But then Lawrence called me at the office the next night. He'd do it. I called Sarah up. "Lawrence says yes. I love you!" I shouted into the phone in my brightly lit Condé Nast cubicle, otherwise stranded in the dark.

Sarah and Lawrence and I were ready to move. That was the best thing about getting him onboard in a way: the ability to start speeding back along. Because at a certain point, despite our ambition and drive, Sarah and I had started to feel that we were wading through water, not air, that every step had become less like sprinting than trudging forward. I think it was because we'd been doing it all ourselves. Because until Lawrence, we hadn't been able to delegate, or rather we hadn't been willing to. *Bleach* was ours, and we weren't going to give it away. And on the one hand we could handle it, in fact needed to be overloaded by it to be fully engaged by it, but on the other hand it had led us to almost implode and lose traction. We'd become so consumed by the importance of what we were doing, speaking only in hushed tones about *Bleach* when we were in public, for example, because we were terrified someone was going to beat us to the punch to creating such a magazine, and also obsessing over things and consulting about them with each other so incessantly, that we'd begun to get in our own way. The magazine had become so important to us and we loved it so much that it was almost as though we had to kill it.

But with Lawrence, whose artistic notions we implicitly trusted, we had to loosen up (and we were also, no doubt, simply getting tired as the months dragged on), and we started planning our fashion shoot. It was shot by a guy named Jude, who'd done things for *Spin* and other downtowny magazines, and it was styled by his girlfriend Agnes, and featured a bunch of girls whom we peripherally knew, mostly friends of friends. We headed out to the Jersey shore in a couple of beat-up vans for the day, and scouted locales as we arrived. Agnes dressed everybody in hot fuchsias and cold turquoises and we started by posing them against the beach boardwalk. At one point, the entire procession of us—the real-girl "models," Jude, Lawrence, Agnes, Sarah, me, and a few others—were called out to by some beer-drinking guys who were sitting on their porch. We stopped and started talking. And we ended up doing the bulk of the shoot right there on their lawn—a campy dream come true that had its own blow-up kiddie pool—and tossing a few of the men into the photographic setups themselves. Liesl, a shy pretty girl who was a baker and who had an edge of the bad girl about her, sat on a little raft drinking a Pepsi and gave the guys and the camera a sneer. Jude clicked away. Later, we found an equally great setup: Further into town, our fashion designer friend Marisa sat on top of a trash can in an electric red dress, and Jude shot up into the sky, transposing her with the building above, which bore a red neon sign that read "Fahrenheit." It was Sarah's favorite. The girls looked like aliens, New Yorkers transplanted into the real world. We had gotten what we wanted.

Driving home that day from the fashion shoot, though, although it had gone well, I felt nearly disconnected from my body. I'd brought along my childhood friend Jesse, who was visiting from northern California, and was three months pregnant. We had gone to Montréal for a couple of days beforehand, and we'd stayed with some of her relatives, whom she'd moved in with for a time during high school. They lived in a big wooden house on a quiet tree-lined street, and they had known me, a little bit, as a child. They were a family: Paul, the father, was a teacher at the local high school, and Kathlyn, who'd been Jesse's stepmother at one time, took care of the kids—at this point just the youngest, Nina, who reminded me a little bit of myself, of what I might have been like at her age, six or so. Nina was funny, and I didn't usually hit it off with kids at that time in my life, but I hit it off with her, and Jesse and I took her to an amusement park during our visit. Every night, we also helped Kathlyn and Paul make dinner.

They didn't know what I did in New York, and even after we explained it to them briefly, they didn't care in any particularly extreme way. They remembered me from before. They remembered me as a child, and oddly, ironically, it made me feel like it was time to grow up in a way that planted the seeds on some level for that to start happening. Because it made me feel that I was simply me, an individual, a person, not a job or a series of accomplishments or a sequence of events. They were a family, and they treated me like family too. It was something I hadn't been exposed to in a long while. It was like being reminded of something, a far-off memory—that was the shape that visit took in my head. And then, in the midst of it all, late one Montréal night after Jesse and I had come home from a bar where we'd met up with a couple of old friends of hers from high school, I had looked out the window of the room I was staying in and thought about going up to the very top of the building and jumping off the edge.

It was the culmination, I realize now, of something that had been going on for a long time. For although Sarah and I were making our two worlds meet on the page during the year we were putting *Bleach* together, I also felt more alone and behind a screen during those months than I had ever felt before.

I didn't leave New York in the end because I was scared we wouldn't succeed. I left because I was scared of succeeding. But I don't mean that in the usual sense, not in the sense that I couldn't accept it, or was afraid of my own greatness. I was afraid of my own predictability, and I was bored by it. I was afraid of what I knew would happen happening. I was afraid of living a life that so many others were already living, and of doing it well: I was afraid of having a house in the Hamptons, and of hanging out with the people that I already knew I would start hanging out with. It would be the people I'd been watching since I was a little kid, or the latest versions of them: people I'd now met, however peripherally—the Kelly Kleins and the Anna Wintours and the Peter Beards and maybe even the Tina Browns of the world. I would be creating myself in their image. In a way, after a while, I figured, why do it? I knew that world so intimately from afar, I'd had my nose pressed up against the glass that looked into it for so long, that actually living in it— joining the party—seemed almost redundant. Or perhaps the truth was that my little glimpses of joining the party had left me feeling the same way that I had always felt just watching it. Even when I had joined—at those parties, holding down that job, at the stray fashion show or starry lecture or reading—I al- ways still felt the same. The outside had changed—I was there, it was real—but inside I had a feeling of inherent distance. It was because I was playing a role. Maybe everybody else was too. It was because I was doing and being what I thought I wanted, not what I felt I wanted.

So I decided to leave New York. Condé Nast pulled out one last stop: A woman in human resources called me and said she thought I should meet with Joe Dolce, the then-editor of *Details*. I agreed; I wasn't so steadfast as to be able to resist this and, in fact, was a little scared that if it went well this editor would make me want to stay. I waited in the lobby of the downtown Condé Nast building that morning, just days before I was flying home, and Joe asked me in. He was in his mid-forties, and exuded the sort of friendliness people with lots of power can afford in New York, and which was sharply tempered by his position. I felt, throughout our meeting, this power he had, but it also didn't affect me as much as it would have a month before. If he had decided to shut me out at any point—if he'd decided he hated me, say—I think I would have even been oddly grateful. I hadn't designed the meeting to impress him at all: I hadn't brought anything—no resumé, no clips. And I told him within minutes of my arrival that I was moving, and I also confessed, with a smile, this fear I had that he was going to say something that would make me change my mind. He smiled back, and said he thought that what I was doing could only help my career in the end. Getting out of New York was always good for building perspective, he told me, and would make me a better editor if I decided to return. He'd "dropped out" himself and gone to Europe for a couple of years, he added, and thought it was among his smartest moves. Then he leaned back in his chair and crossed his arms behind his head.

"How old are you?" he asked me.

"Twenty-five."

"Wow. You burned out fast," he said.

Thinking about it now, years later, what Sarah and I were doing with *Bleach* was, in some very specific ways, a political act for us. But, of course, it was also more than that, more than simply standing up for girls like her and me who didn't have the perfect magazine. *Bleach* and its creation, I now think, were the confluence of two girls meeting, two ambitious and angry girls, two girls who felt the culture weighing down on them like a vise, forcing them to become women in the culture's own image, and two girls trying to make their fantasies their realities.

And it was important, I think, that it was two girls, not one, that it was both Sarah and me. Because from the beginning, I believe we recognized something in each other. I had never, and still have never, met anyone who so completely reflected the kind of drive I had at that time, and the kind of drive that I can tap into even now, although on some level I am afraid of following it too far again because of its capacity to burn me. From the moment we met, maybe, and certainly from the first couple of months of our friendship, we recognized each other. We were both looking for that transcendence through professionalism, and we were both obsessed with transforming our lives. That was what the allure of media was to both of us. Like I said, we should have been the people up there on that panel the night that we watched Tina Brown and the others talking about celebrity, because we were fixated on it. We were famished, somehow, to know what the other side was like. We wondered how fame would change things for someone, how "the other half" lived, what transformation *was*. And we were not only curious, we were unstoppably energetic in our quest to find out what success in any form was like. We were, as I have said, in our twenties, and we were ready to take on the world. And we did so every day in a way, walking home together, talking about how we were going to ascend, how we were going to become editors in chief. It was a time when we didn't understand how some people stopped before they got to the top. We marveled at editors who got off track, at girls who had babies or people who went freelance, or who stayed for years and years in the executive editor second-in-command spot. We wanted power. It was exhilarating, and it was simple. The plan was: We would cut corners, and we would sprint up, up, up. So it isn't surprising then, that after a year or two on the career track at traditional magazines, we got bored.

Doing *Bleach* began as a way for us to go further, faster down this road to success, but it also ultimately became the track that would lead us off of it. It was both a way to get ahead, and it gave us license—indeed, called upon us—to critique the road. It wasn't hard for us to do, because women's magazines were far behind where we were, *who* we were, and we knew that we might be considered the "elite"—the kind of magazine we'd do might only appeal to more urban girls, and stay at a boutique-level circulation of a quarter million—but we believed there was a place for our vision, a place for us in Media Land. And the fact that it didn't already exist not only gave us an outlet for our ambition, it gave us an outlet for the thing that gave us our ambition—our anger.

For we were angry. The truth was, ambition became anger, and anger became ambition in the force of a split second with us—it was a two-way street where the two things mixed and collided and were inextricably linked. There were chains and a certain logic to it all: the chains of anger at my life, and at myself, and at the media—and the links to ambition that came out of wanting to change all of those things. There were vicious circles within circles. And at some point along the line in New York, I knew that ambition had *become* anger. For a long time, I wondered when it had happened. But the real question, I now think, is, was it ever anything but?

Because we weren't just angry about how media treated women, we were also—and had been for a long time—angry about our daily reality. We were angry about all those nights at bars when we felt invisible; we were angry about having to look at all those women in fashion layouts and having to—or wanting to—read in magazines about ways to become more like them; we were angry that we were covering these things and not living them; we were angry at living in our world yet wanting to transcend to the other. *Bleach* was our chance to merge the two: It was our chance to create a fantasy world—a world on the page—in our own image. Before we had it, we didn't have anywhere to direct our desire. And that, I think now, was much of the fear that I felt on those certain early mornings before work, groggy and unthinking but suddenly terrified as I looked in the mirror. *Bleach* was enough to consume us; it was larger than we were. It was a mission.

And once we got rolling, we were unstoppable. It was intoxicating at times and suffocating at others. For we had recognized the ambition in each other in a way that gave us something we hadn't been able to even articulate our *need* for before meeting: It was as though seeing ourselves in each other validated that our particular species of ambition indeed existed, it wasn't just in our heads. And furthermore, *we* existed: *We* weren't just inside our own heads. She had my ambition, so it was real. And with that distinction came a conflagration of sorts—because our ambition was to transcend, it was that much of a burning inside of us, and we egged each other on to do so.

The project itself did too, in both a direct and an indirect way. Not only was it an avenue through which we could let our ambition and energy go, but it was an impulse—this letting our drive combust—that doing the project made us fluent with and which gave us so much of a particular brand of satisfaction that we let it run wild in other aspects of our lives as well. It felt, this energy, this drive, like power in a way. And it was power, inner power, a welling up inside of us of something that might not be girly, but that would not be ignored. It was, as the band Veruca Salt sang at the time, the "Seether": "I tried to keep her on a short leash/I tried to calm her down/I tried to ram her into the ground, yeah," this riot-grrly duo sang, one of them a former Barnard classmate of mine turned sudden rock star. And we, Sarah and I, sang along: "Oh, she is not born like other girls/But I know how to conceive her. . . . Seether!" A friend of Sarah's had told us that the song reminded him of her and me. And he was right; he who hadn't even felt the full force of it was right. For our ambition and our anger were things that we felt and expressed in those days as a sort of wall of sound, and a wall of sound that could be accessed by upsetting us in any way. It could be a boy or a colleague or a girlfriend even: Cross us, and you would be hit with the full fury of it, although the form it took might be oddly professional. We would express it to you as though it were almost emotional martial arts, swiftly and quickly and effectively. I went on a business trip and became involved in an embarrassingly fascinating game of cat and mouse with an older male magazine colleague that I then, upon my return to New York, boiled down into a simplified essence of sexual harassment. I never spoke to him again. I also considered filing a lawsuit, but didn't, for the brass tacks reality was that I would hurt myself more than I'd hurt him. That was part of the streamlined technique—do it, but only if it can be clean. No room for messiness in such situations and relationships: Solutions had to be sharp and immediate, done with perfect mental technique. It came to me naturally in a way, this sort of behavior; it was a small slice of myself that I let grow and thrive, my fury and my drive. And so: chop, slice, and dice. When Natasha wouldn't refer me to her father, a lawyer, when Sarah and I needed free legal advice in the midst of the Fred debacle, I told her I didn't know who she was anymore. "I don't respect you," I said, annihilating our friendship in a way so concise it felt sickly satisfying. In therapy, I told my psychiatrist matter-of-factly on more than one occasion (although always inwardly hoping against hope that she would steer me toward another solution, or at least make a stab at throwing one out there), "I just won't be comfortable in the world until I'm a big success." I won't be successful, I meant, until I'm untouchable.

This overflow of energy—call it ambition, anger, a cocktail

of the two—came out in destructive ways between Sarah and me as well. In later versions of the initial fight we'd had before we'd really known each other, I came to see that in some instances, our shared ambition was almost too much of a good thing even between us, and I remember a time when Sarah and I ran into Elizabeth Wurtzel at a party, and she became angry when I began talking to Elizabeth and didn't immediately call her over; Sarah thought I was power hungry, and trying to squirrel away my celebrity contacts. Or when we were shopping for food for our fashion shoot, the way we wrestled over who would buy what. We were fighting about something else in those moments, something beyond just the surface issues, but I never knew what it was. Now, though, I know it was control. In the end, we both ended up with a surplus of it. In my case, it was in fact my undoing.

Because by the time I left Manhattan, it had become almost like I wasn't only controlling and creating *Bleach*, but like I was also controlling and creating my own life in a certain image. But controlling things didn't work as well with life as it did with the magazine. The catch was that the image I had created my own life in was only of the depth of the page, one-dimensional. For the values that I had come to live by in New York by that time—the things in me that were being fed by that city— were just that, one-dimensional, and the terrible thing was that I had started to notice. I didn't want to notice, it fucked up my life to notice, many of the people around me didn't seem to notice (or else simply didn't get close enough to this stuff to notice), but I did and it scared me. I felt like a film director might who has suddenly discovered that he can direct his own life, and not only that but who simply finds he *is* directing it and he can't stop. At first, it might be fulfilling and exciting—a dream come true in a powerful way—but soon, I wager, he would be scared by his own power and, finally, come to the conclusion that he is living the wrong kind of life if it can be so easily manipulated and triumphed over by the superficial, the planned. He would come to realize that, or at least suspect and be frightened by, the idea that he wasn't directing his life, but in fact his life had *become* a movie. And a movie, surely, no matter how entertaining and magical and real it had looked to him as a kid or an aspiring film student, isn't as rich as life itself. It's more controllable and safer, but it isn't real. And so that is what it felt like was happening to me: I had, finally, achieved some semblance of living my life in that other world, and I was even beginning to reshape that other world in my own image, yet it felt like I was living in a magazine layout. And I was a girl in a picture, who I was watching. I thought she looked pretty good, but I knew, slowly and then finally, that she, by definition, in that format if you will, felt absolutely nothing.

We'd finished the prototype in early December, just days before I left the city, and I remember my favorite thing about it was, ironically, the dummy type. I had written it one morning, another *Bleach*-filled one at work, quickly, and it chronicled, in short little sentences, one girl's story. It followed her as she got up and began her restless day—as she dialed the phone, checked her answering machine, lit a cigarette and then put it out, sat down at the typewriter. And it kept following her—as an elevator door shut on her hand, as her heels clicked on the pavement, as she picked up a penny for good luck. Finally, after pausing at a newsstand, she felt something in the air, some sense that she was looking for something but, as I wrote, "she doesn't know what 'it' is." I made "it," in the dummy type, *Bleach* magazine. "She found it," I wrote, as I had her plunk her coins down and buy it, buy the pages printed with our words, buy the entrée into our world.

And so that was what we had printed all over our prototype anytime we needed words. And I know now that, at that time, that girl was me and she was Sarah and she was every other girl we suspected was out there, wandering those same streets. And I still do hear her shoes, hear them sometimes in my head again, and I even recently had a more violent vision in which they figured, the one I've written of where I pictured kicking through the glass of a television screen in them, cutting my legs on the glass, bloodying my career-girl body and my skirt and my shirt and my shoes. But what happened after all of that in this vision was that I gathered myself together again, once I'd finally made it inside the magic box, and I stood up and kept on walking. And the heels started clicking again: slanting, touching down, sharp, serious, funny now, even glam in a weird way, but mainly just forward, always forward and forward again, into everything, and then finally crashing on through to the other side, outside of the magic box once more. To me now, this sound, this click-click-clicking tells a story: It is, I can hear faintly, the story of ambition, mine and hers—this girl in the heels'—and Sarah's too. And by listening to it over and over again, I can make it out increasingly—it gets louder and louder and more details emerge. Until finally, it is the story of two girls seeing each other—seeing each other's drive and trying to create something out of that combined energy. It is the story of how they kept banging so hard on the door of their fantasies that they did, in fact, finally break through to something real.

the bounty boys

When I think of the boys, I think of the bar we all hung
out in—the Bounty, with its red leather booths and
ship's porthole–shaped windows, and its bartenders who gave
the girls KitKats. I think of the Bounty's scrapbooks full of Polaroids that all the old-time staffers—and they were all literally
old too, shockingly so to our twentysomething selves—kept of
life in the bar, and I even think of a few of these old-timers
themselves. There was one man who used to be there nearly
every time I went in, and he was amazing looking in that way
one sometimes comes across in L.A.: He seemed as though, if
he hadn't been a movie star way back when, he should have
been. He appeared glittery, humorous, *cinematic*.

But, of course, it's really the boys I remember most of all.
For they dominated the bar scene, and I hung out with them for

about six months during my first year in L.A. It was an odd time for me, as I'd just left New York and then Los Angeles too, having spent my first non-Manhattan summer in London. But now I'd returned and was on the lookout for my new life. At the Bounty, I felt I was beginning to find it.

The first time I went to the Bounty was long before I'd met the boys. I remember spending a New Year's Eve there once, and doing ecstasy for the first time, which was sold to me by a very good-looking guy named K. He was selling it to us all in Flintstones vitamin–like capsules—or so it comes back to me now (perhaps it was just a regular pill he handed me, and it's the drug's impact that makes me think of candylike things). But I also quickly left that evening, heading off to a private party for midnight and ending up at a ridiculously heavy metaller–filled fete at the Château Marmont. That year, I was also still living in New York and was only in L.A. for days, so although I remember the bar was pretty and sweet and old-fashioned in a way that was striking for its authenticity (in later years, a Beverly Hills, 90210–hot Tori Spelling would hold her birthday there, having caught on to its unhip-hip factor), soon it slipped off my radar.

But I went back. I went back a year or so later, after I'd moved to L.A. and in a series of nights that, while precursing my involvement with the boys, were a sort of primer in the scene anyway. I found out about the bar during this time, and it intrigued me. It had, in a Hollywood of yesteryear, been a very happening place, one of my friends told me. It was right next to the Brown Derby, an infamous golden-age-of-L.A. restaurant that still had its awning out but was now a nondescript flower shop. It was also across the street from the Ambassador Hotel, one of the grandest hotels L.A. had ever seen, and the setting for many a legendary party (years later, while reading Fitzgerald's *The Last Tycoon*, I would have the hotel brought to life for me in a way it never was then, when an encounter involving love at first sight, glamour, and power took place in its ballroom). But as with the Brown Derby, the Ambassador was no longer really in existence. Although it was visible in disrepair behind a huge wire fence, the hotel had closed down after, among other things, Robert Kennedy had been shot there.

But perhaps the biggest thing I began to know during this time was that the Bounty was connected to an apartment building next door. This building was called the Griffin, and the Griffin was where all the boys lived. And while this might have simply been good news style-wise—the Griffin was huge and regal, and each night when I drove toward the bar, I liked looking at its neon green sign at the top of its skyscraper height— its attachment to the Bounty would turn out to be key news too. Because it meant the Bounty was a *downstairs* bar: If the Griffin had been a hotel, the Bounty would have been in its lobby. This meant that when the bar closed down at two, the party could continue in one or another of the boys' apartments; it meant they were indeed a *scene*.

But I still didn't know the boys. But then one night Kyle noticed me. Kyle was one of the few boys I actually had known about for a while, because he was not only the social ringleader of the group at this particular bar, but he was charismatic in a way that reached beyond the Bounty: He was the kind of guy who seemed to know everyone and be everywhere at the same time.

And I wasn't sure why he began to flirt that night—perhaps it was that I'd recently returned from Europe and had a newly cosmopolitan flair; or that my hair was, finally, long and looking the vaguely seventies-ish way I wanted it to. Regardless, Kyle looked directly at me and smiled, and said, "Hi." And that actually is *all* I remember him saying in those first minutes, but it was enough, because it was never the words Kyle said, but the way he said them. With that single syllable, he communicated a seductive nonchalance that held the promise of further adoration, and a sweetly laconic interior life, and the idea that he was simply too *tired* to say more because he was so busy lusting after me. It was effective. In a poem I wrote about the encounter later, I not only said the evening was romantically rainy—it's possible in L.A., but doubtful—but that Kyle's eyes were like "blue stars."

And after that, we ended up going to his apartment at the Griffin—not only Kyle and me, but a group of us. And while I spent much of my night talking to Kyle's friend Matt, a boy who, while not immediately attractive, had a certain sloppily masculine cadence to his features that I liked, it was Kyle who cornered me outside his bathroom later and got my number. And I was happy. And I was also, of course, on my way to becoming a member of the scene.

But I didn't become a part of it immediately. For a time, my interaction with the bar and boys still centered on the odd night when I'd drop by with other friends, mainly a girl named Zoe, whom I'd been close to since Barnard and who was a part of the scene but not deeply integrated into it. But it also centered, after that night, on my interaction with Kyle. We started playing a nonchalant-on-my-part game of cat and mouse in which he called me, often, in the apartment I was temporarily living in with a friend.

"What are you doing?" Kyle would say in that special way he had; he might as well have said, "I love you."

"I'm eating corn flakes," I'd reply, after a while just making up the most mundane thing I could to see if he might work harder.

But: "I *love* corn flakes," he'd say back to me, charming as always, and I'd smile at his very laziness. And then we'd descend into a sort of Gen X Mamet play. And although we'd hang up soon after that, we'd do the same thing later that day or the next one again. And I continued to become intrigued with Kyle and the rest of the boys.

And then Zoe became involved with Adam. Adam was sweet, and the sort of cute that attracts you when you're in your twenties—handsome, but in an arty and angular way (the perfect subject for an avant-garde fashion photographer—or the new face of Prada, say), and the kind of guy who's always playing some exotic set of third-world drums in his otherwise empty living room, and has dogs in his house and lots and lots of people in it too, and is incessantly offering you hard alcohol, straight. Zoe saw him one night in a diner, drinking a whole milkshake in one fell suck, as it were, and she knew then and there: She'd fall. (What she hadn't realized was that he was likely simply starving, as he was out of work and, financially and lifestyle-wise, little removed from being a street urchin. But in those days such things only added to his allure.) Their first kiss had been horrible, but their second was great.

And because Adam was a part of the Bounty boys scene, Zoe and I started going to the bar more often—and also with more connections. I began to get to know Kyle better, and also the other boys—Robin and Ty, Lou and Ray, Matt. And I started having fun with them. One night, Matt approached me and sat down tipsily at my table. "I wrote eighty pages of a screenplay last night!" he proclaimed in the sparkly tone of a dare. "Do you want to see them?" He motioned up, toward his apartment at the Griffin. I laughed, but thought: Okay, why not? (After all, eighty pages *was* impressive, and he was kind of cute.) So I followed Matt up to his lair and, although he couldn't find the pages and soon apprised me of the fact that he was thinking of making a pass at me (I was taken aback by his forwardness), it was funny. And other evenings were too: I'd talk for hours with Robin and Ty, two sweet boys who would tell me about things like their latest excursions to Vegas, and we'd play games in which we acted like we were different people. And my flirtation with Kyle also took on a new velocity during this time. He had just as lethal a faux-vulnerable edge in our "live" interactions as he had on the phone and we were beginning to really like each other.

And soon, before I really knew it, the whole setup became surprisingly magical to me. I thought it was reminiscent of— even as this sounds faintly ridiculous to me now—what the art salons in Paris in the twenties or thirties might have been like (I'd read about those in Gertrude Stein's *The Autobiography of*

Alice B. Toklas during my recent European sojourn). Because it was that bohemian and entertaining, as Kyle said things that were so oddly yet undeniably bright, and Matt pitched me great scripts he wanted to pen, and Adam, a would-be band member, held forth on the intricacies of music in a way that was captivating. Even the shabby-chic *look* of the Bounty began to delight me—the particular glamour of the bar's red leather and dim light.

But there was also something more. And while it was hard to pinpoint this thing at the time, I now realize it was that the Bounty boys embodied a sort of *carpe diem* aesthetic and philosophy of life in my eyes. It came out in funny ways. One night, I'd ended up talking to Matt again, and he started telling me odd things. He told me that he'd been engaged to Melissa Rivers, Joan's daughter, until recently, and he told me he had a deal with a major New York publisher to write a novel—and intimated that Kyle did too. Yet then it dawned on me that Matt was lying—that most every bit of what he'd said that night had been white lies, and amusing ones, but they were all mere fictions nonetheless. But then something *else* dawned on me: The lying fit right in to what I wanted in my new L.A. friends. Why? Because it represented people who weren't as serious as my friends and I had been in New York—who even thought prestige, as Matt's tone intimated that night, was *funny*. It also represented people who were letting go; these boys seemed, quite simply, to be living in the moment. And it was not only refreshing to me, but it seemed to feed a deep need. And, as such, the Bounty and its boys did too.

And I kept on enjoying the scene for a while—the all-the-time/every-night party that comprised life at the Bounty, and the colored cocktails and laconic glamour. And Kyle and I in particular seemed to get close. He was charming: "So," he began once, "I'm thinking we'll get married by the time you're twenty-eight, and have a baby by the time you're twenty-nine," and then he added, "You know, I'm not planning on being an alcoholic my *whole* life." Another night, in response to my idea that we were looking for different things—which is why it would never work out between us—he'd deadpanned, "What do you mean? I'm looking for casual sex too." It had made me laugh, as so many other things did as well.

But then a few things began to concern me. The first thing occurred while I was being flirted with by Lou. Yes, flirted *with*—I wasn't flirting back—but Zoe hadn't noticed that subtlety, and said I should go for him. But suddenly I felt repelled. And I didn't know why: Was it because Lou was a musician, so too arty for me? Or that he talked about places like Guatemala and things like organic farming, and I found it annoying? Again, I wasn't sure, but another afternoon around this time, a similar feeling hit me when I was with several of the boys at a pizza parlor, talking. While all we were doing was talking, though, it was talk that went on for hours. And although I'd often engaged in this sort of endless talk with the boys, it alarmed me in the same way: I felt repelled.

But I just let it pass. Oh, I thought, I was probably having a relapse into my old New York snobbery, or being too reactive against my hippie background. After all, these people were different from the sixties types I'd grown up around: There wasn't even such a *thing* as a hippie anymore. It was 1997, a different time, and everything was fine.

But such moments continued, and they also began to concern drugs. Of course, the extra drink here, the special way Kyle had of only drinking red wine, the joint passed around at the end of an occasional evening were all an indelible part of the atmosphere I was having so much fun with at the bar. At first, such substances even added to the scene's allure: I remember being high and gazing out the window in Kyle's bedroom one night, and thinking the city looked like glitter.

But then one evening everyone was passing something over my head in the kitchen, and I asked Kyle for some of it. And I'd been giggling and trying to be girly and even girlfriendy as he'd said no, none for me, but it had made me uncomfortable. Another night I was at a party outside the Bounty, but again with the boys, and I approached Kyle. Once I reached and tried to talk with him, though, he was mumbling. But this wasn't normal mumbling, not the shy or charming or cute mumbling of a boy who likes you and is trying to act hard to reach and James Dean–y. No, this—as Kyle and I sat side by side on a used-as-a-piece-of-furniture piano bench—was the mumbling of someone, I slowly realized, who *couldn't talk*.

And then things began to go awry romantically between us. Of course, Kyle and I had never really gotten off the ground romantically at all. Our relationship was always, as were so many in my twenties, largely in my head. But over those weeks, our flirting had progressed, and his hold on me had become quite powerful. I thought there'd been a shift in feeling on both our parts.

But then one night I arrived at the bar unexpectedly. I don't know why I did this—don't know if I was bored or suspicious, or if I simply had the feeling that Kyle was, even in his tenuous closeness, floating away. But I dropped in. And there was Kyle, next to a blonde.

I sat down—why overreact? I tried to tell myself—but soon I couldn't contain my inner emotional whirl. As Kyle smiled at and talked to this girl, and finally took a drink of her cocktail, I stormed out. And even as he came to get me and was able to get away with his antics—after I screamed, "Why do you need so many women? We're like spinning plates!" he stopped and I stopped, and he said, "Why don't you just take off your shirt?" and it made me laugh—similar things kept happening. Kyle wouldn't call when he said he was going to, or once, when we were making out in his room, he had to stop every minute or so to do "something" in the bathroom. I never knew what it was. And soon, even though I still liked the relaxed yet in moments flashingly witty way Kyle had about him, I began to get worried. And then things began to go even more dramatically downhill.

The first thing that happened was that I started to hear things about heavy drugs. In a way, I shouldn't have been surprised; I'd heard quiet rumors from the beginning about the boys— that some of them were doing heroin, and that they favored the liquid kind, snorting it instead of shooting up.

And then one night Matt and I had a craving for smokes. So, looking for some, we wandered up to Kyle's place. As we walked toward his door, I remember reading a paper party-made sign across from it: BAYWATCH NIGHTS, it read, and there was an arrow pointing to his apartment. I smiled. And then we knocked. I don't know why we did this; we were sure Kyle wasn't going to be there. But we did it anyway, and it ended up he *was* there. But I just stayed outside—this was only going to be a quick cigarette break—and watched Kyle's cat forlornly walk the hall. Then, though, I heard something going on. The sound was low, but odd. It was the sound of someone—Kyle, I knew—mumbling again. But it was more pronounced this time. It sounded, in fact, like he was speaking a foreign language.

I opened the door and saw Matt searching the apartment, and oddly casually dealing with his friend's state of mind. But I also saw Kyle. And he seemed not only disoriented, but like he'd taken a total leave of this world. It was like watching someone who'd lost their mind.

And yet Matt and I just left, no cigarettes in hand even after all that. But Matt said, in the hall, "See? Kyle's Satan. He's my best friend, but he's evil too." And he was kidding. But it chilled me: The words did, and Matt's follow-up ones did too. "Don't say I never warned you," he'd added right before we walked into the elevator and pressed "down."

And then another thing happened: I witnessed an act of violence toward Kyle one night. He and I had been leaving a Thanksgiving party when I slowly became aware that a van was trailing us.

"Hey," a voice from the driver's seat said a few times, but it seemed Kyle couldn't hear it; he just kept walking. I looked over at the van, though, realizing just a second too late that

Kyle was ignoring this person deliberately. It stopped, and the guy got out of it and walked toward him. He grabbed Kyle's beer bottle and threw it, its breaking shattering the otherwise quiet night. And within seconds this guy had pinned Kyle to the sidewalk. He held his head near the ground and started screaming, "I'm going to kill you!" over and over again. And although he didn't actually start banging Kyle's head against the concrete, for every single second of what must have been minutes he seemed about to.

And I was oddly calm. I was calm enough to open my car door and get in and start the ignition; I was calm enough to lock my doors and listen and watch in silence and stillness as it all went on. But I was also scared—perhaps so scared I couldn't show it: My fear had crossed over into numbness. And then the guy, inexplicably and before hitting Kyle's head against the ground at all, let him go. Kyle got in my car. He was shaking.

And I just began driving toward the Griffin. And as I did, all I wanted to do in those first moments was take care of Kyle. I wanted to take him back to his apartment and sit with him and put him into bed. But I also, in the wake of those initial minutes and hours, felt this event somehow signified the end of my time at the Bounty—indeed, the fact that there would have to be an end at all. Why? Of course, an element of it was drugs—because I did have feelings of, "Oh my god, I'm going to get addicted to, say, heroin if I try it just once"—but part of it went beyond that. And that night's incident seemed to embody why it did, even as I still wasn't quite sure how.

Yet even after that night and premonition, I stayed a part of the Bounty boys scene for a while. I actually got in deeper, finally sleeping with Kyle, but that, unsurprisingly, didn't improve things. It was disappointing, and not only because he was the third person I slept with (the first was the married man in L.A., and the second, a frighteningly princely boy I'd met in England), and the act itself wasn't great—the highlight was Kyle, my first American, proclaiming, "I feel very patriotic"— but also because Kyle dropped me almost immediately afterward. (Even if it hadn't been great, I might have tried again.) He called the following day, but stopped calling nearly completely after that, and he told Zoe that the reason was that he hadn't realized how innocent I was, but I never really knew why. When I saw him again—only weeks later, but it felt like months—he simply said he didn't want a relationship.

So even my attempts to stay a part of the scene alienated me further, and sex with Kyle, in fact, marked the final watershed for me. Because although I tried to ignore even it for a while—"Oh, I don't care about Kyle," I'd try to say and think, and Zoe once said, "He doesn't mean badly. Kyle just loves women," attempting to make me feel better—I couldn't keep doing that. Part of it was that it was so obvious Kyle didn't love women (soon after our fling, Zoe told me of his taking a girl's virginity and doing the same thing to her that he'd done to me), but it was also that sex, in this case, was more than sex itself. And the reason was that I felt it pointed to the same amorphous darkness that that violent night and the drug rumors and all the rest had seemed to. Yet I still didn't know exactly what that darkness was about. But then I started having conversations with one of my other L.A. friends.

This other friend was someone I'd only known since arriving in L.A., but she'd known Kyle and a few other members of the

Bounty boys scene since their college days. So she could put him and them into some context for me—and she did. She told me, for example, that Kyle had been a ladykiller for years, and she also told me he'd been a renowned partier for a long time—throughout his twenties, and he was now in his thirties. She also said he'd always loved his drinks and that, although he'd gone through a period of showing some commercial savvy in the arena of parties—hey, if you were that good at them, why not parlay it into a career?—by opening a bar of his own in the midnineties, it had soon gone into disrepair.

And at first, this all didn't seem to mean much. It didn't even seem like news; it seemed predictable. But then something began to dawn on me. I began to register Kyle's—and all the boys'—*sameness* for so long. Because this girl was referencing, for the most part, many years earlier, yet they were *still* living red-wine but slightly glamorous, dark bar-drenched lives. And that was my most fundamental problem with the boys— and also, I began to see why even the drugs had really bothered me. It was because the drugs were really just an excuse for— a cover for—something deeper. Drugs were simply the thing that allowed them to pretend it was a seize-the-day quality they had, when it was really stay-the-same-for-all-one's-days lives they were leading. They were just the thing that allowed them—although one wouldn't necessarily need such a thing to be so—to be unambitious. They were just the thing that made it possible for them to pretend what was going on was fun and light when what was really going on wasn't those things at all.

And I also saw that that was why all of those instances— even the earliest ones—had hit me so hard: moments like the one with Lou, and when I'd been talking with the boys that day outside that pizza parlor. Why? It wasn't only a certain ineffectuality portrayed in those instances, and a certain darkness too, but it was that all of it pointed to a deadness. Not a literal deadness, but an emotional and experiential deadness. And it was a deadness, I realized, that if I myself wasn't yet a part of, I soon would be—or would have been. And I began to see *that* fear most concisely summed up by that violent night.

Because that night not only portrayed a violence I felt was at the heart of the scene, but it also portrayed my role in it. For I was not only a girl who thought she was going to a party but who found herself out in the cold and with a guy who was getting his head bashed in—or who was bashing his own head in, as one who thinks he provoked it might put it—that night, but I was also that girl my whole time at the Bounty. I was a girl who was scared and didn't know what was going on and who didn't know where to go during all the months I was a part of the scene. And I was also, toward the end, a girl who was sitting in the car of her life and letting it idle.

Yet now I began to see it, and also began to realize my other, and final, problem. And that was that the boys were poisoning my idea of youth. Yes, youth—because that was what they'd initially seemed to embody to me, along with all the rest: They'd seemed to be experiencing *youth* in all its glory. But now I realized they were not only nearly too old to be doing so (Kyle, again, was in his thirties), but they also weren't doing so in any deeper way anyway. The staying in one place and the zoning out were the opposite of youthful energy and life. And although I'd taken a different turn with my life when I'd left

New York—and was ready to open many different doors—I knew what I really wanted to experience *was* youth. I didn't want to hide.

So I left the Bounty and its boys. I left this bar with its red leather booths and scrapbooks full of Polaroids, and its staff who'd bring you a sandwich, late, if they liked you. And I hit the streets not only of my new city, but also of my new life— the one I wanted to create. And I went on looking for myself, my next friends, my Los Angeles. And although there's no particular night I can remember as being the final one on which I left the boys and their bar, in my mind's eye I see myself speeding home during that late and last evening, passing the blurring neon signs of a middle-of-L.A. night. And although I don't know exactly where I'm going, I'm going there as fast as I can.

thursday night

There aren't many things that spring fully formed right out of your imagination and into your life but, for me, "Thursday Night" was one of them. By Thursday Night, I don't just mean a day and a time, I mean a social gathering which came to be held that particular evening every week during one of my years in L.A., and which was my entrée into the kind of social life I hadn't had in a long time, if ever. But I had always wanted it.

Throughout my twenties, there have been a couple of recurring images, and one of them has been an image of myself, walking down a street in a big city alone. It's something I've tried to figure out what to do with—starting movie scripts with this girl wandering, trying to figure out what she's thinking and what she means—but I've never quite been able to. It's an image that's affected me, though, sometimes in good ways: I've had a couple of people refer to me as a Holly Golightly type since I was about twenty-five, and I always took that as a nice spin on things, my boyfriendless but urban reality. But mostly, in recent years I've wanted to erase the image, because what I came to think it meant was that I was alone, somehow, irrevocably and completely, for the foreseeable future. I came, finally, to see that the flip side of the Holly Golightly thing had always been this darkness, although in some ways I never fully realized it until one night in L.A. I mentioned it to a roommate of mine when someone had said it again, and she said of the complimenter, "You know why he sees you that way? It's because you're single." And I knew then that I didn't want to be that lonely girl anymore. Even if she was, as I'd always somewhere deep down pictured her, Audrey Hepburn, in a long black dress, standing glitteringly-sadly outside Tiffany's eating and looking at diamonds.

That, in large part, is why I had left New York in the first place. I was alone, I would call my mother and tell her tearily, and I feared I always would be. L.A., at first, had been different, consciously created as such, but after a while it seemed I couldn't escape it even here. I had come to the West Coast and thrown myself into social life—and men, and relationships, and sex in particular—with the explicit notion that this was my new job. And I had become involved with what I found around me: A fortysomething movie producer turned lamp salesman who took me to places like Musso & Frank's and the Pasadena flea market and who wanted to discuss Philip Roth at length; a group of almost ridiculously unambitious people my own age, mostly guys, who'd created their own little world around an old-Hollywood bar called the Bounty; and various other friends and scenes that I'd happened upon too.

But nothing ever stuck. Although I'd met and immediately fallen in with the lamp salesman/producer—a month after we grabbed a cup of coffee at a bar one day on his break, I was living with him four days of the week—after three months or so, we broke up. I also didn't want to hang out with the Bounty boys after a while, for obvious reasons.

Although it sounds odd in a way, I now see these entanglements, these groups and people, as social experiments as much as anything else. For they didn't have what I usually look for in friends, subconscious though it may be: They didn't reflect me at all. Instead, I was conscious that they reflected things I knew nothing about. And in fact, the attraction they held for me had been just that—the unfamiliar shape of their lives—because for a long time after I left New York, I wanted to change. And to do that, I thought I had to hang out with what I sincerely called "regular" people: People who didn't have book deals or movie passes, people who liked to talk for the sake of conversing, who did drugs just to pass the time, who were, as John Lennon sang, "watching the wheels go round and round." I wanted to learn from them. I wanted, for a couple of years after New York, to be with them because, as I realized one day with an almost physical clarity, I wanted to put my feet back on the ground. After a while, I did. These people didn't really change me that much in the end, but they did help me to begin to go somewhere else. The problem was, not long after I met them, I always felt alone again.

I can't remember the first time I went to a Thursday Night, but I can remember the first time I was invited. My friend Laura, with whom I was writing a script, told me to come by the Château Marmont around ten for a drink. A bunch of them had started meeting up most weeks and it was fun, she said, but added with the snobbery of a fellow Barnard girl New Yorker, it was becoming kind of an "industry" thing, with all these young execs who'd heard about it running around. I thought it sounded like an interesting evening—"suits" included, and even perhaps especially (fodder for a fiction piece!)—but I never went because, I told myself at the time, I didn't really have anyone to go with. Of course, I could have simply gone with Laura, but I didn't feel like it. I was going through a difficult period professionally—I'd had a column abruptly cancelled, and I was trying to break into a new echelon of journalism where I would be writing full-length features about subjects that challenged and excited me. So far, I wasn't having much luck. It was a period where I found myself waking up in the middle of the night thinking about credit card bills; where I would, a couple of months into it, cry if even the smallest piece was killed; where I found myself short of breath on the phone with an important editor. So I wanted to be alone. I didn't think I could fake it to the degree that made going out fun in my state: I didn't think I could go out and fall into that happy mode of having a drink and liking myself again and letting go. I didn't want to be standing in a corner alone at a cocktail party with a drink in my hand.

Over the next several months, though, Laura brought Thursday up a couple of times again. But I never went, until finally one night I did, and I think it was the evening right after an afternoon when, as we organized three- by five-inch index cards, each scrawled with a scene from our film, Laura told me there was someone she wanted to set me up with. His name was Jonathan, and he was an old friend from New York. I was lonely, so I went. That night, "Thursday" was held at an L.A. outpost of a New York restaurant I'd been to a couple of times when I'd worked at Condé Nast. The West Coast version was an expensive Vietnamese restaurant downstairs, done in a sort of greenhousey style with a white-with-flecks-of-dark-green color scheme that was at once stately and very L.A. It was almost Eurotrashy, and so, it made sense, the two other times I'd been to this L.A. outpost had been with Englishmen, once with a guy I'd briefly been seeing, and once on a semi-setup with someone I'd immediately pegged as gay but then regretted it when I'd read about him and his fortune and his ancient family castle in *Tatler*. "Fuck! That could have been my life! I don't care if he was a fag!" I'd shouted laughingly to a girlfriend transatlantically about it.

Upstairs, where Thursday drinks were being held that week, was darker, all palms and maple-colored bamboo and amber dim light. The mellowness of the décor countered the energy among the crowd, which was a mass of strategically exposed skin and clinking glasses and skinny cigarettes and late-night white noise. Laura and everyone else were near the back wall and spilling out onto the adjoining terrace. In a crunch on the way outside I'd met Jonathan, briefly and awkwardly, but that I remember now only as an afterthought; it certainly wasn't what the evening was about. I also met a lot of other people: Toby, Samantha, Lynn, Ben.

Toby, I remember now, made me laugh. When he heard someone say that I was always dressed in black, he told me quietly across the table what he surmised I was thinking: "It may be all black, darling, but it's all incredibly expensive." I not only thought it was funny (and was, in the case of at least one garment, completely true) but I also thought it was flattering. The others I recall now as bare impressions. Samantha is a flash of blonde; Todd was a blur, always rushing, moving to get a drink at the bar, returning only to alight on a conversation a moment at a time, often to say goodbye, and then only to reappear. But I had the sensation even that first night that I've learned to be grateful for socially, which is that I was interested. I wanted to get to know them all better. The night, to me, was relaxing somehow, like diving into a pool of tropical water.

I have felt this sensation before. I felt it in New York, once, when I first met the group of literary guys I'd ended up spending lots of time with at parties there. Stumbling upon that little scene was like stumbling upon a lucky social wrinkle in time almost, or like tapping a vein. In subsequent weeks, as I'd gotten to know the people who were a part of that scene, a subculture of its own really, many nights had turned out to be almost magical. There's something about being part of a group of kindred spirits, a whole group of people that you not only like but that you also aspire to *be* like in certain ways, and who seem to, amazingly, feel the same way about you. They saw me how I wanted to be. And at first, it was like looking into a mirror that reflected me back, only better than I thought I really was.

A couple of months after I'd encountered this scene in New York, though, after the initial blush had worn off, I'd felt an odd sense of disconnection, like I was allowed to be part of the group only to the degree that my almost-belonging made me more aware of the reality that I was shut out of it. I felt like window dressing, in a way. It was a feeling that grew out of little moments and details, and I still remember many of the specific instances in which it arose: at a book party for a friend, when I gave him flowers and he accepted them with a smile, but barely a word; hearing from a friend that she'd run into one of the guys in the group at a coffee shop and tried to have a "real" conversation but that she'd stopped when she'd sensed palpable fear on his part; having a relatively intimate brunch with about seven of them and, after one of them had asked me a direct question and I'd begun to answer, having him turn away.

Such moments of not belonging were so blatant as to be unmistakable, but they were almost too blatant to be real as well. I was hurt, but I was also amazed, and after a while I began to think that maybe it wasn't about me at all. In the end, maybe the sort of disconnection I felt was of a piece with relating to a group at all, as opposed to simply an individual. I wondered if the feeling of being shut out in my interactions with these people wasn't the consequence of meeting a scene's members all at once, and of falling in love with them all as an entity, of falling in love with them as though they were of a piece so immediately and quietly, instead of having the usual meet and greet

get-to-know-you that one-on-one interactions are made of. I
didn't know. Whatever it was, though, it had all, in the end,
ruined any feeling of camaraderie I'd had in the beginning, and
had made everything seem fake. No longer were we reflecting
each other's best selves back to each other, like the perfect mirror I'd pictured in the beginning. After a while, my social interactions with this New York group were more like looking
through a window into my own social life, like observing it
from afar, as though it weren't mine at all.

I went to Thursday Night again, and after that I had a crush:
Jonathan. He hadn't made much of an impression on me the
first time around, but we'd run into each other at a party one
weekend soon after, and together had descended into a sort of
tequila-induced madness. I remember running around the
house we were in that night—a house so big that the only
black member of the scene that evening had proclaimed, upon
stumbling into the backyard, "This is like Puffy's place in the
Hamptons"—and handing each other lemon wedges to toss
more down, and me, silently, thinking we might make out
later. Then I remember heading to an after-hours club to do
coke. Natasha, who was driving that night, and I were game,
but after circling around and around a couple of blocks of
downtrodden residential Koreatown, we realized we were officially lost and sped home.

The next morning, serendipitously, Jonathan came in to
have breakfast at the same trendy spot Natasha and I had cho-
sen, and I blushed a little at the antics of the night before. But
soon I relaxed and we started talking. It turned out he'd gone

to Princeton, and now he was writing scripts, one of which he'd recently sold to a movie star's production company. "What's going on with it now?" I asked, and he replied in charming around-the-block Hollywood-ese, "It disappeared between her silicone breasts, and has never been seen again."

Afterward, we all headed out to our cars, my feeling that familiar tingling of crush-induced uncertainty and delight. Jonathan stopped in front of his. It was an Audi, a new one, black. Suddenly, I was surprisingly, even to myself, desperately thankful that we hadn't driven my car, which was a '77 Volvo station wagon, complete with extensive outer-body rust and hot air rushing in via the former heater/air-conditioner portals. It also had one of its radio speakers ripped out, where there was now just a gaping hole on the inside of the passenger door. Instead, we'd arrived in Natasha's '85 tossed-around Honda, which was in bad need of a car wash. Not great, but not as bad as it could have been. It was an L.A. moment: My car is me. Thank the Lord I didn't drive it today.

And so the social masquerade began. Of course, it had already subtly begun even before the Audi moment. It had started, in fact, when I'd first met everyone in my expensive clothes minus my hastily valeted car. And I wasn't the only one either: In this town, my girlfriends and I knew, if you had great clothes and made someone else drive, you could achieve a financial façade almost criminally easily, so we did. And we succeeded to a degree that sometimes even made us giddy. I remember walking in Beverly Hills with Laura one afternoon, both of us twinly clad in heels, sunglasses, leather jackets, et al., with her swinging a Tiffany's bag (she'd just charged a present for her boyfriend, which was necessary but had to be done on her all-but-maxed-out Visa). She remarked as we walked, as though reading my mind: "No one knows we each have about five cents in our bank accounts." We both laughed: We *looked* like a million bucks.

Looking like that, appearing to be that kind of girl, was important to us, especially at this time and this place in our lives. No doubt, it had something to do with hitting our late twenties, edging toward the unspeakable-at-that-point thirty, and suddenly feeling like we were expected to be adults. The ones who were able to seem that way, even by virtue of family money and inheritances, suddenly had an edge. Because a lot of the stuff that had been "cute" at twenty-five—the sleeping in a loft area on a futon instead of in a regular bed in New York, the total lack of regard for anything domestic (and therefore the lack of any need to buy anything remotely related to one's apartment, including furniture)—all seemed somehow immature now. No matter that poverty's sudden lack of social acceptability was coming at a bad time for many of us. For me at least, it coincided with my reaping the often difficult consequences of my mid-twenties decision to chuck the corporate security I'd been trying out in favor of a more fulfilled, creative, and financially suicidal route. We all wanted to be growing up beautifully, to be having a nice life, to be *progressing*.

I started going to Thursdays regularly, and while I found out that everyone was a lot like me—dropouts, in a way, but dynamic ones—no one really seemed to be the worse for wear. Luke had nearly finished his Renaissance literature Ph.D. thesis at Cambridge, but then realized that he really wanted to be an actor (something he'd excelled at in high school and college, but never thought to go for wholeheartedly), and had flown to L.A. He was now supporting himself through commercials, and writing material for a stand-up routine. Samantha had been a junior editor at an art magazine when she'd been spotted at a party by a CAA agent, who'd told her, as she now humorously relayed, "I know what a star looks like, what a star sounds like, what a star smells like, and you're a star!" and signed her. She had moved out to L.A. and even in her difficult current situation (she made her money doing extra work) exuded gutsy abandon at every L.A. turn in her butter yellow Ford Fairlane. In the backseats of cars, people would whisper to me that they thought it was "going to happen" for her. And it was true, you could just see it, as she held a bunch of us captive one night recounting, in her southern tones, the story of her moving from the little town of Suffolk, Virginia, where generations upon generations of her family were born and raised, to the big city of Manhattan, à la Eliza Doolittle. She seemed, quite possibly, a star-in-the-making in moments like that, as she did when she showed up at a party another night in full Miss America regalia, an outfit she'd apparently been wearing to her first stand-up gigs recently, where she portrayed the icon slowly and then crazily as a messed-up girl who ended up railing against the audience.

A sizable number of Thursday-goers were doing even better, seemingly skipping that difficult proving-ground time to be embraced professionally already. Ben, who had won a student Academy Award for a short feature he'd made while at film school and, also based on its merits, been summoned out to L.A. by a famous film director, had just inked his first deal to direct. Rob, who'd left a letter-perfect life as an American-in-England Oxbridge grad, seemed to enjoy the same effortless ease in the wake of his decision to "go Hollywood"; after he and his brother, Laura's boyfriend, Scott, had started writing a comedy script, they'd almost immediately become darlings of the industry screenwriters.

And so, one perfect glittering night a week, I got to know these things and more about them. Gradually, we seemed to get close. Over the weeks and then months, we got to know each other's habits. Todd, nearly the only one among us who had a day job, always left early. Gregory, who was putting the finishing touches on his Ph.D. thesis, always stayed late, and then wanted to go somewhere else to do harder drugs. Jacob smoked pot, wandering into that night's scene after a day of teaching poli sci to college undergrads with a dazed smile and just-rolled-out-of-bed hair; Toby, who came from a religious background, didn't get high. We also got to know each other's quirks: Jacob, Laura and I suspected, had been giving both of us the eye. I was pretty sure I wasn't interested; Laura, in a fantasy kind of a way, thought she might be. Luke liked to dance, and we would, like I never had with anyone else, in a little tiny disco bar where power feminist babes moved to the grooves in leopard print lingerie on the stage. There, Luke and I moved in perfect syncopation for hours: Twirling, falling and then being caught, almost falling for each other a little bit after a while. We even got to know some of each other's secrets: Laura, who'd been with Scott for six years and loved him, still wasn't sure if it was right—if they were "the ones" for each other; Jason came from the *wrong* side of his notorious political family; the British Lynn had lots and lots of money ("Can you believe she's so *normal?*" we asked each other in hushed tones).

But we got to know all of these things as facts, not as symptoms or results, not as part of a contextualized reality. We got to know these things, and each other for that matter, as fragments, little slices, in the same shape as our strictly Thursday interaction itself: fascinating in some ways and yet also, somehow, incomplete. Of course, incomplete as it may have been, Thursday was still a good fragment, an almost perfect one in fact. And I needed one perfect piece at that point in my life. I needed that one night out of the week when we'd meet in some expensive and glamorous L.A. bar. Todd was responsible for this setting, in some ways—the one who sent out the e-mails apprising us all of that week's whereabouts—and a couple of us even started to whisper about it after a while, the incongruity of the fact that we were meeting in the lounge at L' Ermitage, a hotel whose multimillion-dollar renovation had been chronicled in that month's *Vogue,* or in the bar at the Four Seasons, or in the back at Pinot Hollywood, where we'd sip ten-dollar drinks on couches and talk the night away when many of us could barely afford groceries. But we never did anything about this incongruity, and the truth is we never really wanted to. Because although Thursdays was in certain ways absolutely out of many of our ranges financially and had little to do with our current lifestyles, it was where we gradually, over the months, came to define our future lifestyle. It was almost like a once-a-week affirmation, the valeting and the cocktail glasses and the dressing up and, after a while, it was how we saw ourselves. Thursday became the night when, no matter if an editor had killed a piece of mine, or if I had no money for rent and was charging food on a credit card (in fact, perhaps particularly at those times), I'd still turn on my *Last Days of Disco* soundtrack or my Air CD full-blast and throw on my Italian black boots and my Barneys black pants, paint on my bit of mascara up close in the mirror, and blend in my foundation until I looked flawless.

And I would drive to that night's bar. And as I think about it now, it seems fitting to me that it all took place in a bar. For I have spent some of the most interesting, real and unreal, hours of my life in these places. Bars have been, to me and to a lot of other people I have known in our twenties, the places where we have grown up and experimented with who we've wanted to be in large part, the best places and the scariest places and the most unpredictable places of all. Now, looking back on those years, I picture myself almost running through them—on my way to my future, most definitely and desperately—in different cities. Hotel bars in New York—ones with ripped velvet seats, old and authentic—and recently renovated ones in L.A., with white chairs and expensive skylights going to waste, looking up only into the starless city nights. Smoky, divey versions and honeyed, hip versions. I've been seduced in them, had men kiss my hands and sweet talk me in them, and even, occasionally, laid down on their couches with some stray cute guy when we were too drunk to think. I have fallen into lust in them, felt like myself in them, felt more alienated and out-of-touch in them than I have in any other place. I have been in bars so dark that the light looked black, and I have been in bars so crowded that I was pressed up against total strangers for hours. I have been in bars that were like funhouses, on weekend nights walking through masses of drag queens as a disco beat burned through us all, and I have had the most intimate dates of my life in them, in my own little made-up world with someone else. I have broken up with people in bars in Hollywood and I have gotten to- gether with people in bars in the East Village. I have lost my- self and found myself, in a way, in bars.

It's something about the drinks and the darkness, I think, the way a smooth cold cocktail becomes a seamless seam to a beta state, and then you're just a hop-skip-and-a-jump to something else: bed maybe, but more often just a dream of what you want to be. And everyone else around you changes too, really and falsely, they shift—visually and mentally, they shift. Entering a bar for me, one where I know a lot of people especially, has always been a release, a sort of giving up to something else. You get a drink with a little bartender repartée and suddenly you're there, talking and flirting and being who you wanted to be all day but who you were too tired to even re- member. "Hey," you say, and you're off, floating on a raft of words and glances and sounds and alcohol that makes you give up and forget all the rest. It's the last stop on the way to your dreams, the place where you don't know what's going to hap- pen next but where you feel so safe that you're okay with it, where that golden boy in the corner is looking at you. It's that in-between place, the middle where it all meets, where the drunken fantasy meets the real reality for a couple of hours.

And sometimes, it's even the place where who you are and who you want to be not only meet but finally dissolve, the edges between the two blur and then disappear altogether. Of course, it's not really real, but it's a break. And it's a balance to achieve this right feeling, this feeling that you are who you want to be, it's a balance of alcohol, of the room, of the people you're with, of what you're wearing, what happened to you that day, your dreams and fantasies. But when it works, it works, because somehow in its fakery it's so fucking close to being authentic that you don't even care that it's not. It's night, it's so dark outside that you can't really tell what's real and what isn't anymore, everything is faded, everything is black, everything that happens within those four simple walls isn't really happening in the usual controlled and difficult way of the world. In a bar, the effort goes away, and your only job is to fall. And so you do, and even though in the morning it's all over and you're back in your room again, you're refreshed in some psychic way, and ready to try again in the real world. So that's what Thursday was perhaps the apex of, the swan song of, as we all headed ready or not into our thirties. It was a continuation, in some new and improved way, of all of those other nights, in all of those other cities, in all of those other bars. Maybe, this time around, I would get lucky and find what I'd been looking for.

And then I failed. I had gotten an assignment from *The New York Times Magazine* to spend a week in Mexico at a psychology conference and then to write it up as a three-thousand-word feature. I left after the first of the year, and while I felt that I was in over my head once I got there (these academics literally

spoke a different language, I would tell friends when I got back),
I also knew I had a good story.

Returning, I'd pitched the basics to my editor, who'd cut me
off after fifteen minutes or so of excited explanation and told
me to focus on the science of this movement rather than what
I thought was the deeper story, the cultural implications of the
scientists' ideas. I said fine; I was just delighted to have the assignment. I thought this shift in focus would work itself out, as
creative things, if you stick around long enough, usually do.
But writing it, I'd had to keep this editor's advice in the fore-
front of my mind—focus on the science, and position that itself in the middle of the piece—and fight the voices that told
me otherwise. I tried to follow her advice anyway, though, and
I hoped it worked.

I got a call about a month after I'd sent the piece in then (a
not entirely unusual time frame in the freelance world), and it
was the editor. She said that she was sorry, but the piece wasn't
going to work for them. The science of the movement, she
said, just "wasn't there." She was very nice about it and I was
very nice about it back, and then we hung up.

Then I started crying. I couldn't believe it. Beyond the me-
chanics of it—two months of my life gone, and one polite
phone call in explanation—the piece had come to represent
something more to me than just a story. The New York Times
signaled I had arrived in a new way. The New York Times meant
my life was moving forward, that everything was working out,
finally. I kept crying and called my mother. I was confused, in a
daze, and my parents were furious—furious at the nonchalance
with which the piece had been dropped. And then I called

Laura, because I had to about something else, and when I mentioned it to her, I surprised myself because I was, in a way that I hadn't been with my mother, terrified. "Do you hate me?" she reminded me I had asked her during this phone call, when we were talking about failure and success months later in a casual conversation. I was embarrassed at the memory, as I had been at the time, and the truth was I barely remembered it: I had blocked it out. But the answer to that question was, no doubt, at that time what I truly feared. I feared that Thursday Night was just an illusion, wasn't meant for me unless I was the big success they all were or were at the very least going to be, that it wasn't real somehow, and if I became real myself in that worst way—through my own veritably gravitational failure, which I'd run from for so long in New York and thought I had finally given up running from in L.A., but suddenly had something to lose by—I would lose my life. I would lose my friends. And I would lose, in a way, myself.

Laura, of course, reacted with sympathy and disbelief at what had happened, and said no, of course not, Straws, it has absolutely nothing to do with what I think of you. I know you're talented. You don't have to tell me; I'm the girl, she reminded me, who called you up last year and told you that my book deal had fallen through. And it was true, but I had just forgotten it somehow; it wasn't how I thought of her. Then we both began wondering what this feeling I was having, and that she'd had similarly when the book thing had happened to her, was: Why do we all feel like we're going to lose everything personally if we fail professionally? We thought it might have something to do with our parents and that, regardless of what it had to do with, it was fucked-up and off-base and untrue. Later, I talked to Natasha and she had an even more radical reaction: "Listen," she said, "when something like this happens, it makes people like you *more*. Not less. They feel like you're human. You were too perfect before; it makes everyone feel like you're like them." It made me feel better, but I was still scared. I still hadn't told anyone from Thursday.

Over the next week, I went to a party, this one with Natasha and Todd and Luke. It was a TV party, filled with network people, and we didn't know any of them. I didn't know exactly how I would portray the *Times* thing, but I didn't really analyze the presentation of it either; it was never, even in my turmoil, a matter of being anything but straightforward. So at one point, as we all hung out relatively alone in a room off the main party area, Luke asked me about it. And I told him. I didn't cry about it; I think in fact I probably laughed about the fact that I had cried. I told the others, gradually, too, over the course of the next ten days or so. And what I found was amazing to me. What I found was that just as discovering Thursday Night at all had been like tapping a vein, failing in the full eyes of the group was like tapping something just below the surface too. A couple of people, immediately when I told them or in the days afterward, confessed to me that they'd failed as well.

Luke, over drinks late one night soon after the TV party, at a bar on Beverly, said that he hadn't left Cambridge at all. Then he told me the story of how he'd run into complications regarding his dissertation. He had been the "golden boy" at school, he said with humor and confusion and sarcasm. His supervisor (or "advisor," as we call them in America) had loved him, but suddenly, when he'd been close to finishing this last monumental project, the tone of one of his meetings with her underlings had shifted. It was during an oral exam when they'd questioned him about his topic and point of view in a way they never had before, and he'd realized nothing he could say would change their hostile stance. While he wasn't sure why, he thought of several things, among them the fact that, in his first year, his supervisor had invited him to her country house for the weekend. Luke had been uncomfortable because she'd had a reputation for seducing students and, although he hadn't felt any overt shift in that direction, he'd decided to leave the country early. Could his examiners' criticism be reflecting a desire for revenge on this woman's part? In the end, the why of it all didn't really matter, though. His examiners suggested he go for a lesser degree, an M.Litt.

Luke was devastated, but tried to recoup. He'd been wanting to act—in some small but clear part of himself he knew it—so he got on a plane and came out to L.A. But he found himself feeling that even the smallest chores—picking up a cup of coffee, getting out of bed—were incredibly taxing. It was as though his life were taking place in slow motion, as though his brain was a wilting plant. The only way he'd snapped out of it was by going into, first, therapy, and then onto antidepressant drugs. "You know what it was like?" he told me when I asked about the feeling of Zoloft. "It was like my brain was being watered." I asked him how long he'd stayed on it. It was an uncomfortable moment. After telling me he thought it was a small price to pay to never feel that way again, he said, "I'm still on it."

I had similar moments with other members of Thursday over the next couple of weeks. And I wondered, during this time, why we hide from each other the very things that will bring us closer. For I got to know these people better because they shared their failures in response to mine: Ben confessed he had been working at a casting agency before he landed his deal to direct, and that it had made him so embarrassed that he'd tried to keep it a secret from the rest of us. Rob, I heard, had been thinking of moving to Europe, because the most confusing thing of all had happened to him: His success *felt* like failure anyway. He'd discovered, through his writing of several scripts and doctoring of countless others, that the isolation of writing made him lonely to the point of despair. Samantha felt like her self-esteem was being torn to shreds by her extra work, and sometimes wondered how long she should give it. Luke, another night not long after the Zoloft one, told me something else too: His parents had recently staged a "career intervention," as he put it, because they were worried that their brilliant son had gone so rapidly from being a rising academic star to someone who was grateful to be in the final running for something like a Burger King commercial. This last thing I couldn't help seeing the humor in, picturing Luke's family sitting around him in a circle, telling him firmly and earnestly, "Honey, you're hurting yourself, and you're hurting us, with your Hollywood aspirations." It sounded, ironically enough, like a great scene in a movie. But although this last Luke revelation was funny to me, it was fascinating and touching, like all the rest, too.

So we became real. I became real and, instead of evaporating, they became real as well. And it began to cross my mind that maybe, in fact, it had been me keeping everyone else from getting real in the past, in those other groups, in the end. I don't know. But the amazing thing about it to me was that instead of being a roadblock to the group or making it fall apart, our realness made us closer. It actually was the thing that made us into a group at all. Because it made the group necessary to us: Suddenly, we needed each other. We weren't just people who hung out at a bar one evening a week together, trying to valet our screwed-up cars as discreetly as possible before dashing in in our fancy duds. We were friends. For even though they'd all seemed so glittering to me, the truth was we were all, to varying degrees, alone: Rich or poor, ascending or not, we were almost all professionally freelance, and personally single.

We were all edging toward thirty, too, without the family and kids that some of us had been taught to expect by this time, but even more than that, without the sense of being adults that had been implicitly promised us. None of us felt like adults. And it's something that I've still rarely heard acknowledged, but that I find to be almost frighteningly true: No one ever tells you that you're never going to feel grown-up. That it doesn't happen. That you do get older but that you don't in a way, and that you're just supposed to act like it's happening, even when it's not. And so the group became that for us: the place where we could get what we needed because it wasn't happening, and the place where we could fake it that it was; it became the place where we could look at each other as the glittering successes that we wanted to be, but also where we could peer behind the curtain and find that the truth was nothing like that at all. It became the place where we could be each other's illusions, and then, after we finally admitted it, where we could be each other's realities too.

Thinking about all of this, I realized it was a feeling I'd had before, coming home from a California vacation once where I'd spent time with a group of people I'd known intermittently, during holidays and in different cities, for years. I'd gotten to know them better over that particular trip, though, and suddenly, on my first night back in New York, I noticed that I felt safe and happy thinking about these people all over the other coast who were eating dinner now, who were watching TV at the same times that I, in what felt like my own little world, was doing the exact same things. I felt like I'd belonged then, and through Thursdays I felt like that again. The difference was, now it wasn't from a distance.

Life is a process of elimination, someone said to me recently. After I laughed and told this person that that was a cynical way to look at it, though, I realized that in some ways it's true. Except, I hope, it's just so horizontally, not vertically: I would like to think that by ruling out some of the vastness, we get to hone in on what we really want and go deeper. The months after the *New York Times* thing felt like that to me. For I don't think the people I met at Thursday Night drinks just happened to be the people I had this breakthrough with. I believe I had this breakthrough with them because they were the right people for me. They were the people who I saw myself in, for whatever superficial reason initially that turned out to mirror something in both them and me more truly.

What made us into a group, finally, was the two sides of

this: the fantasy and the reality we were able to identify with in each other, the stark terms in which we were really living softened by the particular and similar dreams we all had. It allowed us to be, in a meaningful and understanding way, right there with each other, through both each member's failures and each member's successes.

One night the summer after Thursdays had started, we all went to the premiere of Scott and Rob's first movie, a picture they'd directed—not just written this time—about growing up. We all gathered in the secluded area behind the theater that evening: Laura and Scott arrived in a limo, Samantha came in her Fairlane, I drove in in my station wagon.

After everyone had arrived, we walked together through a tunnel, and out the other side, at the end of which was a crowd of unfamiliar but enthusiastic people and the famous red carpet and cameras. "The red carpet!" Natasha and I pointed out to each other giddily; we were about to, albeit anonymously, walk it. It was the kind of scenario that's so famous that once you're there it doesn't really seem like it's happening to you. Scott and Rob went first, they walked into the lights, and were instantly enveloped in a burst of flashbulbs and mikes and energy. We all followed in the background, without a nod from the media but with a thrill all the same. And it was a thrill we felt that whole night, a thrill at the real and imaginary experience of it, at the blindingly bright cameras and the jostling microphones and at the speedily fun after-party and at the famous people and at the regular people. A thrill at seeing our friends pull it all together and create something out of a vision that in some way all of us had. For me, I know, it was as though that evening, the real and the dreamlike, the day and the night of our lives, the aspirations and the reality that we'd all grappled with for so long finally met.

And it wasn't just about the cameras or the glamour that night, although it was those things too, it was about having it be ours, all of ours somehow, knowing it had risen out of what I knew to be the nonglamour and the hard hours and the endless days of working and wondering if what we were all creating was worth anything at all. It was as though all that time we'd been posing a question to the world and that night was our answer. It felt complete. *I* felt complete. How would I explain it? I didn't know. But days later, sitting at my desk, I saw that girl again. That girl in my mind. This time, I managed to follow her. I watched her. She wandered for a long time, and then she walked into a bar.

I met Sam the way I met a lot of people in L.A., one night at a bar with friends while talking and sipping a drink of some sort, probably a vodka cranberry but maybe a gin and tonic or a cosmopolitan. It was my third year in the city, and that night I was with a group of most of my friends there, a group made up of New York transplants like me. We'd come to L.A. looking for a way out initially, not just out of Manhattan, but out of everything that city represented—the ambition, the power, the *fever*. We'd come to L.A. looking for a place that still ran on adrenaline but where if we wanted to stop the professional world and get off, we could. And for the most part, we'd found it. We'd also found, with relief, each other.

And so Sam was the latest. He'd just arrived from Manhattan and a job in the art world, and I can't remember if I

thought he'd actually moved here or was just visiting. I can remember that he had dark brown hair and pale skin and was
wearing black, and although he is very good-looking he didn't
initially strike me that way. Instead, he struck me as being occasionally loud and funny, and as someone who said things you
couldn't predict. I remember looking at him as he was sprawled
almost rudely across a couch, and that he reacted by asking me
if there were any dance clubs nearby where he could go do
some good drugs. So he seemed funny (he was obviously kidding about the drugs), but he also seemed anxietized, like
someone who's not quite sure what's happening and who wants
to cling to something, anything. I got the feeling the side of the
couch in the bar that night might even do. But mostly our interaction was uneventful: We flirted and talked, but about little things, nothing major, and even most of that turned out to
be untrue, white lies on his part. Afterward, I still had no idea
of what he had just gone through.

   Over the next few months, though, I would come to know
that Sam had just lost everything, and had fled from it all, too.
He'd taken a plane to L.A. in a panic several weeks before we
met, having left his wife because he was afraid he'd never find
happiness with her, and also because she'd wanted to have him
hospitalized for psychiatric problems. This latter thing was an
unfair and frightening betrayal on the one hand, but, as I got to
know him, a valid if panicked response to a real problem on the
other: Sam, who'd been diagnosed as depressive in his early
twenties, had been having more serious problems with his
mind recently. I, oddly and without even knowing it, identified.

But that night I knew none of this, and we just flirted. At one point, someone sitting on another couch started trying to plan a surprise birthday party for a mutual friend whom we all loved and hated in a way, and whom Sam had come with that night. When they asked us if we wanted to come, Sam said his name loudly.

"Jack? Jack's an asshole," he said only half jokingly. I thought it was a little mean but fun, more fun than anything that had happened in the last couple of minutes at least. So, he told the truth. Because Jack was, in a lot of ways, an asshole. But you wouldn't really say that kind of thing anymore, except maybe in a bathroom at a party to a girlfriend, or on the phone, or to someone who didn't know him just to qualify his personality quickly. No, you wouldn't say it loudly and in front of everyone like that. We were, after all, in our late twenties, and plain old mean-spirited babyishness wasn't something that was really allowed. But, of course, we all still felt it.

The birthday ended up being planned anyway—the comment was pretty much ignored by the fervent friend—and Sam and I just kept talking. He told me he was getting a divorce, and that he'd worked at a gallery for a couple of years but that he was coming out to L.A. to make it big in the entertainment industry. He said this last thing with a mixture of sweetness, fear, and egomaniacal abandon. To me, it was charming. And then he returned to the dance club idea. He said he actually was meeting someone at this place called the Blue, and did I know where it was? I'd never heard of it, and it crossed my mind that it might not even exist, but I didn't question it too much. I just told him that there was another club he could go to down the street—when you're tipsy, a dance club is a dance club. He said it sounded good and that he needed air, and then he walked out alone onto a quiet strip of Sunset, and into the night.

I didn't see him again until a friend of a friend's housewarming party a couple of weeks later. Sam was there because he knew the girl who was giving it, and I'd been brought by our friend Todd, who was the social ringleader of our group for this particular couple of months. In the meantime, I'd gotten a bit of background on Sam. He'd been the one several people had been talking about at a fancy dinner a couple of weeks before— the one they'd been discussing because he'd gone "crazy" and started lying about who he knew and what he was doing. He was the one they kept trying to tell they'd still love even if he wasn't a big success or best friends with famous people or landing multiple Hollywood production deals, as he'd started to claim. I remembered laughing nervously about this guy when they were describing him over dinner, and adding in a story of my own about someone I knew who'd been friends with a girl who sounded similar, and who'd ended up having to commit her to a psychiatric ward. Realizing that this name-less, faceless person they'd been talking about was Sam, though, was no longer sadly funny. It was just sad and a little unbelievable now: How could the guy on the couch that night be *that* screwed up? But I knew he probably was. So, talking about all of this late one other night with a friend, I made a pact with myself: I was definitely not going to get in-volved.

But then I went to this party. And after saying hellos and taking off my coat and checking out the scene in the living room, I walked outside into the courtyard. Sam was standing there with his dog, Daisy, and a camera. He took a picture of me and a flash went off in my eyes, and then I said something along the lines of, "Hey, I remember you." I was happy to see him. He looked good—in a well-cut but casual suit, attempting some sort of modern Rat Pack vibe that worked all the way down to, but not including, a ridiculous pair of black and white bucks. I began teasing him about them. He took it well, smilingly but somewhat shyly, retaliating with good humor by just taking picture after picture of me as I skipped from that topic to the next, asking him about himself in a variety of ways until we were in what felt like a mental dance. And remembering it now, the whole encounter dissolves into movement, coming back to me in a blur of energy more than anything else: his camera, the flashbulb constantly popping, my self-consciously girly flirting, the smiles and posing, the dog jumping around, and the party melting into flashing lights and sounds all around us.

Of course, as the hours moved on, we were both absorbed into other things. But before the night was over, Sam and I ended up alone again in a little room off the kitchen. I was sitting across from him on a sofa with my shoes off, and talking to him with the sort of animation one exudes when one is around someone they like. He noticed my excitement, but misread it: He asked if I'd ever been diagnosed as manic. Immediately, I knew he was talking about himself, but I answered as though I had no idea. Why, did I seem that hyper? I asked.

Yeah, he said, but in a good way—I just seemed really happy, and it reminded him of how he'd been a couple of months before. It was less a nice thing to say (although it was that too) than a simply intimate one, and it was made more so by my sense of his problems.

The next time we connected, it was at another party, in another L.A. house, another late night. I saw him at a table in a corner, bathed in darkness as the evening wound down again. After eating birthday cake together and exchanging funny small talk for a couple of minutes, I'd mentioned the word *girlfriend* in some sort of other context, and he'd seized upon it and told me that that's what he actually needed. He downplayed it then; he told me that he thought he just needed someone to hang out with these days, someone to be his friend. It was cute instead of pathetic, which is how it might have struck me had it come from anyone else's mouth: Such are the advantages of the incredibly physically attractive. And then he told me he wanted to go, and I offered to drive him home (he didn't have a car or even a license, being a lifelong Manhattanite). As we walked outside together, I was conscious of breathing in the cool L.A. air, and of feeling clear.

We went to an all-night restaurant, and on the way he looked at me from the passenger side and asked, with amusement, if we were going to make out. I laughed and told him that was funny—that it was the kind of thing I was always saying and regretting. When we sat down at a table, he ordered a hamburger and I had a beer, and then, when the waiter had left and we were alone again, he asked me what I was looking for. I asked him right back what he *thought* I was looking for. He laughed. "You want it all. You want everything. You want the fantasy," he said. "But you've been hurt." I thought it sounded pretty trite, and almost felt a little embarrassed for him—I bet you say that to all the girls, I nearly taunted—but I was also halfway taken in. There was something going on with him that night that was at once playerly but also unmistakably raw, and the latter redeemed the former, made it ironic more than anything. So we continued. He said a couple of other things that were both lame and sweet enough that I started to like him again (at one point, he said my "energy" reminded him of Jennifer Love Hewitt) and after we finished our food and drink and were walking out, he proposed that we check out the kitsch-cool motel next door. "Why don't we get a room?" he asked nonchalantly, and I greeted the idea with buzzed delight. We walked like conspirators into the lobby and asked if they had anything: We felt like teenagers. But there were no vacancies.

Instead, we went back to the car and drove to his apartment. When we walked in and turned on the lights, I was surprised by the sheer quantity of disarray he was living with. His place was an amorphous mass of half-unpacked boxes and their tossed-out contents, deconstructed computers, electronic toys, and packets of pills. Sitting on the floor, though, after a minute or so I didn't even think about it. I was nervous about other things—about him and me—and I said so. Sam said he didn't get nervous, but thinking about it now I'm pretty sure that he was. And as he said that, he walked over to a little green Incredible Hulk–like robot and pressed a button on its stand. The toy moved its arms in a greeting motion and said in electronic tones, "Welcome to my terrible apartment." I laughed, and Sam leaned over and started kissing me.

It would be a lie to say that what happened between us over the next couple of weeks wasn't something that I understood or even looked forward to and could anticipate. Because what happened over the next couple of weeks is what happens when you get involved with someone like Sam: We got really close, really fast. I got to know many of the facts, the clean hard bare facts, of his situation quickly and truly, for one thing. And it was information that he imparted with a great degree of charm and endearing recklessness, almost like a charismatic seminar leader, I thought to myself sometimes.

First off, he'd recently been diagnosed as bipolar—"or manic-depressive, either one, they're the same"—he explained one afternoon as he haphazardly tossed me pill bottles after I'd volunteered to help him organize them into little piles. We were attempting to tidy up his apartment, a futile project from the get-go (we took to characterizing the décor of his one-bedroom as "post-tornado"), but one that we attacked with a lot of esprit de corps on that day. And we approached the pill organization in particular with the same lightness and matter-of-factness that we would have any other household chore—organizing books, say, or sifting through files. He would toss me a container rattling with caplets of the mood stabilizer Depakote, for example, and casually ask me if I wanted one, or quiz me on what he called its "mind-fuck" properties. And gradually, through this method, I came to know this: That bipolarity made him really, really happy (or manic) or really, really sad (or depressive), and that the depressive aspect was shared by his mother and brother too, and that it had landed both of them in the hospital at various points.

He didn't want to be on the drugs. He'd try to pretend it was okay, that it was no big deal, telling me that practically every truly cool person was bipolar, and that there was even a website where I could go to find out who—Peter Gabriel, Ted Turner, and there were a lot of other people on that list too, he said. Sam also attempted, it seemed to me, to make bipolarity something more "normal" than it was, intimating on several occasions—as he had at that party—that he thought I might have similar problems, and trying to entice me gently, as I've mentioned, to try a "fun" pill with him whenever I seemed upset or moody. But he didn't take it well when I twisted this kind of jokey talk the other way around, going cold the first and only couple of times I referred to him as being "cuckoo for Cocoa Puffs" or "livin' *la vida loca*," both expressions that I thought were funny and that he'd take in the spirit that I meant them, which was: innocently, endearingly, flirtily. And writing that now, that I ever thought of his problems as a means for flirtation sounds not only odd but also offensive to me, but I simply didn't get it then. Because although on one level I sympathized and even identified with the problems Sam was having, his manic depression was also, to me, in the beginning, almost cute.

Part of this was because he told me a lot, but he didn't tell me everything. The rest I came to learn through experience, through going to the movies and to dinner with Sam, through taking him to parties and being taken to parties by him, through hanging out with him during the day and through driving him home at night, through sitting with him on the beach and waking up in bed next to him in the cold L.A. winter mornings. And gradually, the gravity of what he was dealing with hit me squarely and consciously, and in all its inescapable reality.

These were the kinds of clues. For the first couple of weeks I knew him, Sam's favorite place in the world was Fry's Electronics, a huge hardware store–like warehouse in Burbank. I only went there once with him, but there was something about the experience even then that was off. We got up and after breakfast we headed out there, and once we arrived, he began expertly navigating one of the store's industrial-size carts around, tossing things like VCRs and laser pointers and headsets into it. I got mad after awhile because it was so boring for me, but was placated immediately (and somewhat disturbingly, I thought with amusement) when he tossed a portable CD player in for my stereo-less car and sent me off to buy my favorite compact disc of the minute. After a couple of hours, he finally finished and pushed the piled-high cart toward the cash register. There, I watched him hand the woman behind the counter various credit cards until he finally gave up and went to a cash machine to retrieve the eight hundred dollars he needed. I barely knew him then, but I had the sense that something was terribly wrong. As we walked out, I asked him as lightly as I could if he was going to slit his wrists later because he'd spent so much money. He laughed and said no. But about a week later, he confessed to me during a particularly black mood at breakfast that it was money problems.

Not long after the day at Fry's, he also told me that he was going to be out of town that upcoming weekend, because he was flying to Japan for the unveiling of the latest Sony Play-Station. He said he'd been hired by a friend to photograph the event for the Japanese equivalent of *Details* magazine, and that he'd taken the job for practically nothing, just as an excuse to get out of town and check out the new toy. As the weekend approached, he kept referring to it with tension, telling me that he was worried his parents would try to stop him from leaving the country because they thought he was in a fragile emotional state. But, he also kept telling me he was going to go anyway. When someone kept calling me that Saturday then, leaving mock-prank messages on my machine, I'd still assumed it was him, but that he was calling me from the air. When Sam finally reached me that night, though, he acted surprised when I mentioned Japan. "Oh no, that ended up falling through," he said casually. "So, can I talk you into coming over to my place and watching DVDs?"

And those were just a few of what became countless unexplainable, odd, and finally both manic and depressive moments. Other times, at the end of an otherwise normal daylong date, he would ice me with an oddly physical prickliness, on one occasion running out of my car after stiffly shaking my hand goodbye; or on the phone, when I began talking about myself and friends of mine, he once countered that he didn't want to talk about me or them, all he wanted to talk about was himself. He would disappear without a word for days and occasionally even weeks too, before I'd get a short but affecting e-mail entitled something like, as it once was, "damaged," with a barely coherent apology and a plea for more time without having to contact me. But after the first couple of times such things happened, which I took personally, I learned to react to it all with a sort of clinical detachment, feeling only sympathy where, if anyone else had acted this way, I would have felt anger and confusion. I learned—through the counsel of my friend Natasha in particular, who'd just gotten her master's degree in psychology—to realize that it wasn't fair for me to demand more of Sam because he, quite clearly, didn't have more to give. For he was acting out in ways that were, while seemingly random and even mean-spirited, in fact just classically bipolar: The reckless spending of money, the hot and cold emotions, the lying were all parts of his condition.

Looking back on it now, of course, it all seems plain and clear-cut that this was at the very least a headed-for-nowhere situation, and more likely a guaranteed broken heart, but at the time it was hard to fathom. I think it was because what was simultaneously occurring between us—in the spaces between the lying, the not calling, and the rest—was a relationship of startling honesty and, to me, almost shocking sweetness. Often, this sweetness seemed to be of a piece with his falling apart: the night Sam told me so adorably that he wanted to "disappear" with me at a party, but then I realized it seemed partly because he was in no state to be around people, and he held my hand as though he was holding on for dear life; the times when he'd fall asleep in my car on the way home to his place and I'd watch him breathe at stoplights, so inarguably perfect, but then suspect his sleeping was really just him having passed out because he needed another pill.

So it was complex. And to be sure, a lot of what was going on with him was not just manic depression, but also a naturally extreme reaction to his impending divorce. And no doubt, a lot of what I felt in those first weeks was just sympathy. For I witnessed his pain, its intensity, night after night. The first time was one evening after dinner, when we'd had a normal meal joking and hanging out, but he'd suddenly gotten sad when we'd come home to his place and he'd found a letter that upset him in his mailbox. I didn't know what it was, but I could feel something shift in the tone of his voice and the way he was rattling the key in the door to let us inside. When he opened the letter, he went straight into the bathroom and closed the door. He turned on the faucet full-blast, but I could still hear him crying. I remember the sound, and I felt it too: It was like pain being suffocated, like breath being stopped. I sat in the middle of his living room on an inflatable chair and listened; there didn't seem to be anything else I could do. When he came out, I thought I might cry too. I asked him what had happened. He'd gotten something from Elizabeth, he told me, something he'd asked for but something that made him sad to get anyway, was how he explained it.

And it went on: Another night, we'd started fooling around while watching—as a joke—*WarGames*, but after kissing for a couple of minutes he'd stopped, and asked me what was making me so hesitant. I didn't think I had been, but as we started to talk about it, he dropped his point and started talking about Elizabeth. He told me that as things had deteriorated with her emotionally, sex had gone downhill too, and it had become a source of great pain and frustration for him; he said he'd tried everything to make her happy but nothing had. And he said this with an anguish and a sadness that made me feel I didn't take anything that seriously anymore; he was deeply and darkly consumed by something he couldn't even grasp, it was so big. Sitting there, I don't think either one of us really knew what it was. It made me feel like I'd lost something, though, something intense and painful but that in a weird way I also missed. It reminded me of the way I'd felt in New York after a while, the loneliness that had become my life after the beauty of the city had worn off. It was the way I'd felt in my last months there, before I'd realized I had to leave.

At first I kept trying to solve his problems, or at least begin to figure Sam out: figure out which reactions were related to which issues, which were an expression of a broken heart and which were more than that—an expression of his psychological state. In the end, though, such analysis led me nowhere, because the truth was that it was always a mix. Sam's mental condition and his heart were inextricable. His mental issues, I finally realized as I watched him cry over Elizabeth time and again, were a part of him—a part of him nearly as solid and important, at least in his day-to-day reality, as his heart and soul.

But the problem was, even as I began to see these things and others—all of which added up to a warning sign not to get involved because Sam was incapable of getting involved with me, at least the way I wanted—I was falling for him. And the irony was that the warning signs themselves were the things that were making me fall harder.

The reason for this was that I somehow, inexplicably but deeply, identified with him. I felt it often, and not least in reaction to Sam's most painful moments and memories. During his honeymoon week, he told me one morning as we walked to get coffee, he'd cried almost incessantly. He would often, he said, sit in his and Elizabeth's hotel room during those days and nights, overlooking a secluded and expensive beach as she, "the budding psychologist," as he now characterized her, tried to comfort him. After a while in their relationship, he said with regret, he'd felt as though he'd become her thesis project. I didn't know how to respond to this. But for me, something became silently clear: What he really regretted, I thought, was not so much her making him into a psychological "project" as much as his own mind for making him so perfect for the role. And this was the thing—his betrayal by his own mind—that I, that morning and throughout the intervening weeks, at once completely identified with emotionally and was left completely at sea by intellectually. For to be betrayed by oneself was something that I knew touched me, but that I couldn't quite grasp in any conscious way. It was like trying to watch oneself walk down the street, or instigate an out-of-body experience: Impossible, but somehow imaginable and understandable—if only in snippets, in moments, as ever-elusive mental bits—at the same time.

I can remember the moment that I realized I'd become deeply involved with Sam. It happened late in the game, almost humorously so, and it was one night when I'd already gotten involved to the point that I thought we might break up. We'd gone out to dinner, and it had ended badly, with him feeling stressed about money and getting cold and distant about it. I was of half a mind to leave, but it was late so I stayed. And while he lay silent in the living room, on the carpet, I got up and went into the bedroom. I stripped down to my T-shirt and underwear and got under the sleeping bag that he used for cov- ers. As I lay there, I checked out his bedroom because I thought I might not see it again: I looked at the tossed-around cardboard boxes, the frayed copy of *Premiere* magazine on top of the television, the big old-fashioned camera Sam had bought at a secondhand store a couple of days before. Then I listened to him turn off the stereo and go into the bathroom and turn on the water. I listened to him brush his teeth.

When he came in to bed, he lay down close to me, smelling like Crest and cold water. I could feel him thinking in the dark. I asked him what it was about. He didn't say anything for so long that I thought he might not even answer, but then he turned to me and told me that he just wanted me to know that whatever we were doing, that what we were, us, had nothing to do with her. I thought about it for a second, and then I said that that was nice, but that I didn't believe him. I tried to say this in a light tone, and I wanted to mean it that way. But the truth was, what he just said at once flattered and hurt me, be- cause I wanted it to be true but I knew that it wasn't. And in the midst of this, something wonderfully simplifying hap- pened: Lying there so close to him, I suddenly felt what I can best describe as a magnetic pull toward *us* really, and it was a pull that was clean of thought or hesitation. It was physical, not mental, finally, and it was a relief.

Sam had hung out for several more weeks after that, sometimes almost every day, sometimes not speaking for days, but the very last couple of times I saw him I felt closer to him than I ever had. One day at the beach, he told me that he felt like my presence calmed him, and it seemed almost, as a friend of mine who saw us together around this time commented, like we were becoming a real couple. But then his parents came to visit and he disappeared again, this time contacting me only once more, over the phone, to tell me that they were taking him back to New York. I started out the phone call fine, almost professionally I think now, and the truth was that in some ways his moving back to Manhattan was kind of a relief. But after we hung up and I started telling a friend what had happened, I found myself crying, and then he called me back. Now I was crying in front of Sam, and it was an odd feeling. I felt stupid, I said, I knew what he was doing was the right thing, but somehow it was just heartbreaking to me that he had to go through all of this. And then I said that I didn't know why I was crying, I was just overly sensitive I guessed, and he said he knew, that that was what he liked about me, and then we hung up. I felt sad, but I also couldn't help thinking about how incongruous it felt to have finally cried in front of him. It felt like we had switched roles.

Months later, I was sitting in a diner and I heard a song on the radio. It was an old John Lennon hit about breaking up and, as I sipped my coffee, I began to understand what had happened between Sam and me with a kind of clarity I couldn't get during the thing itself.

To be with Sam, I realized, was to simultaneously experience being without him. To be with him was to lose him. It was the flip side of falling for him, of falling for anyone who wasn't available to fall for me. And he wasn't available because he was too busy mourning his own losses, and that was both the painful and the pleasurable math of our relationship: We were both, continually, in the act of losing and recovering something, and then losing it again.

I experienced this loss every time I walked into his apartment—the apartment of someone falling apart, strewn with DVDs and taken-apart cameras, half-built computers and blown-up "air" furniture. It happened when we'd stand at a street corner in the late-afternoon L.A. sun and I'd see the look in his eyes, the heartbroken and tired look of someone who needed another unwanted drug. It happened when he told me, marring an otherwise perfect night, that he didn't want to have kids because what he had was genetic. It happened when he told me anything about how fucked-up things had been for him over the last couple of years, how his mother had clashed with Elizabeth, and how his brother had spent months of his life institutionalized for depression. It happened whenever Sam showed me the kind of sweetness and love that I wanted to believe he felt toward me but that I knew on some level weren't about me at all because he was still relating to a version of Elizabeth that I had become.

Of course, the irony is that this loss—both my amorphous sense of it, and the literal manifestations of it—was our connection. Because Sam had the same problem, although the particulars were different; he was constantly in a state of losing something too. So we liked each other because we understood what the other was going through. And understanding this called upon something in both of us. It called upon a certain kind of love—an inescapable, unquestioning, and unhesitating all-too-human love, a love that was almost forced out of both of us even in the depths of despair. And while in the end I know that it is this continual sense of pain that took our relationship away, it is also the thing that created it. It was the deep and dramatic commonality that made us, in a sad way, made for each other.

I've thought about why I was attracted to this kind of relationship in the first place, about why this sense of continual losing was attractive to me at all, and beyond that, why it's something I identified with so immediately. For it is something I felt deeply familiar with even before I met Sam and it's also, I believe, why I connected with him from that first seemingly inconsequential night I met him, sprawled across that couch.

I'm not sure, but I think maybe I find an answer when I think back to my own first weeks in L.A., when I'd just left New York and was in a circumstance that approximated Sam's when we were together. Although I wasn't suffering from mental problems in a clinical way, I did feel on the verge of breakdown at that point in my life, and I was also, in a certain sense, suffering from a broken heart. For New York was a city I moved to so young and that I fell in love with so completely that it had the capacity to hurt me badly, and for a long time after I left it I really felt that it had. Because it, or life, hadn't ended up being the particular way I wanted it to be, or how I thought it simply had to be, I held New York accountable for a long time. And when I left, on a plane one innocuous sunny morning, I felt that who I was and who I'd wanted to be had been broken. I felt, flying from that coast to this one—from the East to the West—that I had lost something, and I wanted to find something new. Sam, I'm pretty sure, had had the same thing happen, although with different specifics.

I think now that that was our connection in the most basic way: He was looking to make the next step, to grow up through enduring the breakage of all that he'd cared about, and maybe I struck him as someone who'd already made that leap. And now, looking at it this way, I've started to think that perhaps what he needed in the end wasn't, as he'd thought, a girlfriend, but rather, as he'd corrected himself that night at that long-ago party to recognize, just a friend.

I would have liked to have been that for him, and in some ways I know that I was. But if we'd talked about all of this more directly, which we never did, here's what I might have told him. I might have told him about my own complicated experience of coming here and of leaving there, of going from twenty-five to twenty-nine, and of looking for and in some moments truly finding happiness. I might have told him about the simultaneous sense of unexplainable loss and amazing freedom I'd had for a long time after leaving New York. I might have told him about the kinds of people I'd met out in L.A., who were answers in themselves to many of my questions. I might have told him about the ones who tried to hold on to things, and to gain them: the guy I knew who'd started out as a novelist in New York but who couldn't make enough money there, so was now working for an ad agency and driving a Mercedes bought with the windfall from what he called his "fuck it" job at Grey. And the friends I had whom I'd watched let it all go: the girl I knew who'd lost her boyfriend and her job and her apartment the same week, and who'd somehow allowed that to lead her to begin writing, the thing she'd always been afraid to try. I might have told him about the fact that both of these kinds of people appeared different to me now than they ever would have before, because they never would have appeared to me at all in New York, because I'd been too busy and too sure of myself to even really look or to listen at all in that city. I might have told him about the nights I'd spent in bars with friends here in L.A., and how a couple of times someone had asked me if I was happy, and I'd said yes, and sometimes I'd meant it, but other times later I'd thought about it and decided that maybe it was just numbness. I might have told him about my new city itself, Los Angeles, the place where I'd found all of this and which I've come to think of as the counterpart to the city that broke my heart. I might have told him about reading an interview with Courtney Love in a magazine, and how Courtney, it said in big letters on the bright page, thought L.A. was romantic. At first, reading this, I'd wondered what kind of a fucked-up person you'd have to be to think that, but the comment stuck in my mind, and later—after a couple of weeks—I'd started to think that maybe she was right. And I'd begun looking at it then, this new city, from the windows of my beat-up old car, with new eyes. But it's not romantic in the wide-eyed, young lover way that Manhattan was to me, I would tell him. It's romantic like someone who's been around the block is romantic, it's romantic in its sense of lost and found, in the way that you can come here to give up and some- times you find that that in itself gives you the key to start try- ing again anyway. It's romantic because it's where you come to stop trying to put the pieces together, and sometimes, in your newfound freedom, you solve the puzzle anyway. I might have told him that now, these days, that's how I think of the strange and seeming randomness of him and me.

But I didn't tell him any of those things, and Sam didn't tell me much about exactly what he was looking for, or what was going on in his eyes in those weeks either. Even though I went out with him for a while, and in some very real way fell for him, I was left not exactly knowing what he thought happiness or love or growing up or any of those things were.

What I remember instead is just our simple and inexplicable connection, and in particular one afternoon we spent driving around L.A. together, when he asked me if I wanted to hear about the love of his life. I said I did, and he told me that it was this girl he'd known in high school, and he touched my hand on the steering wheel. "It was this girl I went out with for about a year, and I could communicate with her telepathi- cally," he said. I looked at him, and he was speaking in all seri- ousness, with an innocence I hadn't seen before. "I could just touch her, and she knew. And I knew. It was like we were talk- ing silently, talking without words."

"So *that's* what you're looking for," I said with a smile. He said, "Yeah." Then he took his hand off mine and put it on the warm dashboard of the car.

"Words without the words," I said.

"Love without the love," he said back to me.

As we kept driving, I thought about it. The conversation didn't make sense anymore, but the phrases still seemed to fit together perfectly.

two girls

As I walked down the hall that first day at Barnard, I remember I thought I looked very New York. I was wearing jeans—faded ones, slightly flared—and a black top, one made out of a crepey material that had an asymmetrical hemline. I also remember that I was tired, so tired I was hyper. I'd been traveling all day, flushed with being the young girl in the big city. I'd flown in that afternoon from a suburb of L.A., where I'd spent the summer with my parents. I was nearly twenty, and felt, as I would feel so often during the upcoming decade, that I was starting over.

But now all I was doing was walking down the uptown hall at Barnard, in a building called Brooks, where I was to find my new home. The place was faded and dingy in a way, bookish and impressive to me in another. I looked at the numbers in the center of each doorway, hammered-in brass ones. And then I found it: 305. I put my suitcase down and knocked. A girl came to the door and asked who it was before she opened it. I told her. The door swung open, and she gave me a hug.

Her name was Natasha, and she looked like the prettiest cheerleader in my suburban L.A. high school class: a blond girl named Ashley, who was on the school paper with me, but who never did any work as far as I could tell. Ashley had been the kind of person who was effortlessly cool, and her cool came out of her effortlessness: I'd envied her "over it" perfection and conventional looks. But Natasha didn't act like Ashley. That hug was friendlier than I'd ever seen Ashley be, and it startled me a little but I was touched by it too.

I put down my bags. The room, Natasha informed me, was a single with a bunk bed. "There's a bathroom," she said, standing in the doorway that led to it. I checked it out. We looked at each other: Were they serious? But there also wasn't a lot we could do, at least in that moment. I opened the venetian blinds—let's let the sunlight in!—and began unpacking.

Almost immediately, Natasha and I began trying to improve our lot in dorm life. Our setup was ridiculous, we informed the "housing authority," an office downstairs populated by a man named Tim who was shorter than both of us. "Look, Tim," I would smile, in my first practice runs at being an I-get-what-I-want New Yorker, "neither one of us is sleeping in the bathtub." This was my favorite line. Natasha sat next to me, and we took turns looking alternately supportive of each other and outraged. "We just feel that we're paying twenty thousand dollars a year. Are we *not* paying twenty thousand dollars a

year?" she would ask. Tim would hem and haw but never do
much of anything, except ask us to come back. Which we did.
After a while, though, we began to wonder if he was flirting
with us. The thought made Natasha and me livid, and we'd
come on doubly strong the next time around. We were feminists, we were saying between the lines in these meetings, and
we kept on saying it until we got caught up in the swim of
classes and the city and so many other things in our new lives.

So we stayed in that room, and we began to get to know
each other almost by default. We were both nocturnal, so we
would stay up nights, talking. Natasha had grown up in Rhode
Island, she told me, but the college she'd transferred from was
in the Midwest. It was where her father had gone, but she'd
started to suspect she'd have to leave after the boys began
yelling out their dorm windows to the girls walking to the cafe-
teria, calling them "cows." Things had only gotten worse
when, in her second year, she had starred in a school play and
one night during the run realized she had no sense of where the
screen separating fiction from reality lay anymore. She'd finally
decided to leave the school after her favorite teacher took her
aside and told her she was too smart to stay. "Get out," this pro-
gressive woman said. Natasha, with gratitude, did.

I also slowly told her about myself. I confessed that my
brother and sister had been admitted to a rehab hospital right
before I'd left for New York, and that my parents wanted me to
start going to Al-Anon, the twelve-step program for families
and friends of addicts. She replied that it might be a good thing
for her to check out too. So we both did, albeit separately, and
another night we talked about it. I thought everyone was just

wallowing, I said, my words hanging in the blackness, and I told her that one woman at my meeting had stood up and said, "I've been coming here for eight years, and I still feel like shit." Then the woman had started crying, and sat back down. I heard Natasha laugh in the dark, and I did too. At her meeting, she told me, people had started throwing chairs.

Sometimes Natasha and I would hang out on campus too. One day, as we sat on the steps outside one of Columbia's biggest buildings, I told her that my grandmother was no longer paying for my college education, because a couple of months earlier she'd gotten into a fight with my father and they'd stopped speaking. I told her about my parents too, and that they'd had to get real jobs for the first time in their lives that year, my painter mother working at Laura Ashley in the local mall, and my writer father working as a receptionist at a PR firm. I continued, that day, telling Natasha my father's situation was almost funny, and recounting a story about a short fiction piece he'd recently written about a guy who works at McDonald's and is constantly asking people if they "want fries with that." But the key word there was "almost" funny. My father had laughed when he'd told me about this story, but I hadn't. "I'm the hope of the family," I said to Natasha. It's a comment that stuck in her head more than mine, though. She would remind me of it years later.

But although we were getting along, I was convinced that Natasha and I wouldn't really be friends. It was little things. It bothered me when she'd take a cab to the Village because she didn't feel comfortable riding the subway so far downtown: I'd think, with irritation, about how "bourgeois" she was. Or when she would wear certain garments—horizontally striped tights, *hats*—or say certain things. And I was sure she felt the same way. One day, I came home to find a quote posted on our door. "East is east, and west is something else entirely," it read. It referred, I was certain, to our different coastal backgrounds. Aha! I thought: She doesn't like me either.

But I also didn't really mind what Natasha thought of me, or what I thought of her. I was busy looking for other friends— sophisticated and New York friends. I was prepped for my life to become *Metropolitan*, the movie. It had come out the summer before I arrived at Barnard, and my Dalton-alum aunt had told me that it approximated a particular kind of Manhattan life. It was the kind of life I wanted, I'd decided, and I'd even spent a certain amount of time that last California summer trying to wipe the Valley-girl tint out of my vocabulary to get it. (It hadn't worked: "I just want you to know that, like, I'm *totally* not a Valley girl," Natasha would later recall my saying to her on our first phone call.)

I was still hopeful, though, so I continued looking. And until I found it, I would sit tight. In the meantime, I would pin, as I did, my Sargent poster of *Madame X* to the wall near my upper bunk, and I would go, as I also did, to the Modern and Metropolitan museums in my downtime. Occasionally, I would even have a late-afternoon cigarette on a bench in the Barnard courtyard, delighting in thoughts of what my life was about to become.

But afterward, I would return to my room. And Natasha and I would talk and hang out, and our connection continued to sneak up on us. One night, I went to a bar and did cocaine for the first time, and I ended up dancing with some other students to a broken jukebox for three hours before coming home. When I returned, Natasha was hanging out with her friend Chris, a sunny-looking guy who was visiting from her hometown. I'd assumed she wouldn't approve of my antics, so I didn't tell her about them. But then they'd asked me how to get somewhere, whipping out a map, and I, still high, unfolded it until it stretched clear across the room. After shuffling through the thing, trying to help, I'd giggled. "I'll need to take a taxi to get where I need to go on this *map*," I suddenly yelled, and we all laughed. Later, I told Natasha part of the reason for my late-night ferocity. She'd been cool, and even curious, and we'd stayed up again that night, talking until it was nearly light.

Natasha says the first time she realized we were friends was during Christmas break of that year. We'd both moved out of Brooks, and each gotten what we wanted. I had a single in an old building, in a quad I shared with three other girls, and Natasha had rented a place off-campus, an apartment near school. She was sharing it with two other girls, her friend Elaine—an academically brilliant but alarmingly thin girl who used to drink massive amounts of coffee before going running each day and who, late one night, had knocked on our dorm door and asked if we could spare a couple of rice cakes—and another girl named Skylar. So, that break, I called Natasha up and we talked. It was a turning point, I realize now: It was the first time we'd been in contact voluntarily. I told her about my brother and sister, who were still in a locked facility, and how I'd done group therapy with several movie stars. She told me her parents were getting a divorce.

Over the course of the next year, I would go over to Natasha's apartment sometimes and hang out with her and her roommates in their bright white rooms. Natasha, I could tell, was feeling better than when we'd first met (I'd come to realize she'd been in a depression then), and a humor I'd never known was shining through. "She's a *supermodel*, Straws," she'd say of Skylar when I asked if they got along. It was true—Skylar was Swedish, and had the looks of a blond Linda Evangelista—but it made me laugh. And Natasha would come over to my place too. I had—ironically, considering my postfeminist stance in those days—been put together with three of the most radical feminists on campus, and Natasha knew them from volunteering at Barnard's Women's Co-op. So we'd all hang out in the kitchen, talking about boys and our parents and what we were reading. One of my quad-mates, in a nod forward to nineties Madonna feminism or backward to seventies sexual freedom, took to having an affair with a younger pretty guy we all called the Boy Toy, and he hung out with us sometimes as well. Another of the girls I lived with, Jane, seemed fine until one day she was found staring into space and disoriented in her bedroom and had to leave school.

But while Natasha and I hung out casually and occasionally during this year, I still don't think either of us thought we'd figure in the other's postgraduate life. One night late in our senior year, though, she came over to my room and said she thought we should live together in the fall. Most everyone else we knew was leaving the city, she reasoned, and besides, it might be fun. I agreed. And so, out of necessity and random circumstance, one part of the chaos we knew we were heading into was resolved. And then we graduated.

My first memory of being out of school is walking up Broadway one summer afternoon, talking with Natasha about playing strip poker the night before with a book editor. I'd met this editor at a party, and gone home with him in the rain. He'd had a big loft in a seedy neighborhood, and told me about things like running into Jean-Michel Basquiat years earlier, and having the artist take paintings out of his backpack and unroll them right there on the sidewalk. Natasha was wild with jealousy, although she was trying to hide it, and I was almost jealous of myself I was so excited. I was nearly in love with this boy, I was convinced, and the sun was shining, and we were young and in the city, and we kept walking for blocks and blocks.

I did that a lot that summer, just walking. I got to know every square foot of the Upper West Side after a while, and I liked it. New York, I was beginning to feel, was mine. Natasha and I didn't really know anyone, though, and one night we went to Danceteria with the vague notion of making some friends. We walked in, and almost immediately met two guys. Hers was named Loren and I can't recall the name of mine, but he was blond and the heir to a European beer fortune. That evening, we all hung out and then we dated them for a while, until Loren clumsily tried to seduce Natasha by telling her they were going to a restaurant called "Café Loren," and leading her to his front door, and my guy—despite his charming predilection for biting my fingers at bars—didn't call when he said he was going to one too many times.

But after a while, we found ourselves in a lull, after the thrill of leaving school had worn off and the freedom that was so palpable in those first days and months had too. The summer faded into fall.

That September we moved into our first apartment, in Chelsea. We'd checked out the East Village, but decided it was too young for us (amusingly in retrospect: We moved there two years later), so moved into this place. It was a one-bedroom, just big enough to be considered loftlike, on Twenty-fifth Street between Sixth and Seventh avenues. The neighborhood was dominated by XXX video stores and magical interior-design firms that were in warehouselike spaces and had huge windows filled with avant-garde-looking mannequins and sleigh beds and pop-arty sculptures. I would walk by them every morning on my way to work. I was temping at Chase Manhattan Bank in Brooklyn. I slept in the living room, and Natasha had the tiny bedroom.

Our décor, beyond my futon and her bed, consisted almost solely of a black and white poster of Miles Davis. It was a photo taken by Anton Corbijn, and I thought its high contrast was beautiful, but Natasha felt it exuded a ridiculously heavy vibe. "Look at him, just look into his *eyes*," she'd say. But I would just smile. There was no use fighting over it, even she finally agreed: We had to use what we had. And that wasn't much. I had a Mac Classic computer that I'd placed on top of two trunks, and one day Natasha went to the flea market on the corner and bought a red velvet armchair for twenty-six dollars. I also had a portable tape player on which we incessantly played Madonna's latest, *Erotica*, and after a few months we bought a TV too, as we wanted to watch the presidential debates, which were beginning the night of our purchase. (I'd invited the editor to come over and watch it with us, but he never showed; Natasha and I sat on the floor alone and ate ice cream and cookies and lusted after Clinton instead.) But what we didn't have is now more glaring to me: silverware and pans, a table, dressers, any real chairs beyond that red one.

It was an emptiness and a lack of cohesion that reflected what was really going on in our lives, though. Because what was really going on was that Natasha and I were trying to build lives at all. And it often felt as mechanical and odd as it sounds. I remember feeling this oddness while I was walking home sometimes, returning from another job interview and becoming preoccupied with the idea of needing towels, say, or an alarm clock. Or I would find myself worrying about money in one breath, and boys in the next, and what to eat for dinner in the one after that. I suppose it was just life, but it felt very foreign then—so random and endless and *indiscriminate*. There were so many things we needed yet we knew nothing, or so close to nothing that it still surprises me, about how to get any of it. Pay a phone bill? Clean the bathroom? We—or at least I—really didn't know how to do these things, so often we didn't. Our phone was turned off regularly, and soon our tub was toe-deep in grime. A friend of mine told me she was always shocked at how put-together I looked emerging from my place. "You guys are like kids," she said of Natasha and me. I laughed. In a way,

I thought our nonchalance in such matters—or what looked like that—was great, even glamorous. But what also strikes me now is how, in so many ways, we really were kids then.

On weekends, Natasha and I discovered a cool little bar down on Ludlow Street called Max Fish, and started frequenting it. Practically every time we went, we'd meet someone, and Natasha had a brief affair with a Waspy guy she met there named Marston. I came home one night and he was over, and there were candles everywhere. In the dark, our place almost looked like a real apartment. During the day, Natasha also started taking acting classes with a well-respected teacher. She'd decided to pursue acting again, which she'd done as a child and into her teens, but had opted out of when she'd gone to Barnard instead of doing a Broadway-bound play.

I was looking for a job in journalism, and decided against going back to *The Nation*, where a copy job soon came up. I wanted a different and glossier scene. It was proving harder than I'd anticipated, though, and after four or five months, I felt as if each job interview brought me further unhinged. It reached an apex when I "auditioned," as I'd come to think of it, to be part of *The New Yorker*'s typing pool. "What do you read?" the bookish young woman who headed the department had asked me before administering the dreaded typing test (I couldn't type). It was a fair enough question, but she'd said it in a way or moment when it reverberated to me as, "Don't you read *at all*?" It tapped into my insecurity about not having been an English major, and my deeper worry that I might never garner a New York publishing job. I mumbled something about

Balzac and Flaubert and Mary McCarthy and made it through. But I left her office that day feeling illiterate. For weeks afterward, it seems to me now, although I wonder if it really could have actually been that long, I sat in our red chair and tried to read *The Deer Park*, by Norman Mailer. Natasha took to tiptoeing around the apartment. I was still so tense, though, that I just kept reading the same few pages over and over.

So my identity began falling apart during these months and days, page by page, I almost felt it. And Natasha's seemed to as well, as she went from acting class, where they broke her down emotionally, to auditions, where they did too, and then to her waitressing job. At that last place, she told me, her boss snorted cocaine incessantly and often gathered everyone together to tell them they needed to start acting more like a family. In her despair, Natasha took a stab at writing short stories, one of which made me laugh because she characterized her life as being like a slowly emptying bathtub, with her self getting closer and closer to the drain.

And then one day things came to a head, at least for me. The people at the bank offered me a job. They said they would pay me thirty thousand dollars a year, despite the fact that they'd had to reprimand me for wearing too-short hot pants only days earlier (I had very few clothes, and even fewer corporate ones: Natasha and I were pooling our conservative attire, but it still didn't amount to much). And I had to consider it. Thirty thousand dollars was a fortune to me then—the only other way you could make that was by going to a consulting firm, I thought to myself—and I'd been looking for a job for nearly half a year. I was, as the day went on, progressively torn.

When I got home, Natasha was gone, and I lay down on my bed and tried to sleep. But I couldn't. I tried to weigh things, but I couldn't do that either. I felt trapped, a girl in the body of someone I no longer knew. Natasha came home and I was crying.

She sat down next to me. I told her I didn't know what to do. "I need the money, but I just can't," I said through my tears. And I told her how I felt. How, for the first time in my life, it was just me—I wasn't at a school, or my parents' child, or someone from a particular town. I was in New York alone, without a job or even a sense that I would get the right one anymore. "But I'm not the girl who works at the bank, you know?" I said. She replied that she knew I wasn't. And I believed her. I believed her because she knew me, and because she particularly knew me in this in-between place: She knew who I'd been at Barnard, and who I was looking to become out in the real world. But I also believed her because she was going through the same thing, so realized how dead serious the advice she was giving me had to be. She knew it because she was relying on me to give the same kind of advice to her.

Part of the reason was that there was no one else to give it to us. We were alone, and not just in the city. We were also alone emotionally, and contact with my family at least only made me feel more so. I remember realizing this one Sunday, after walking home in the rain and stopping to pick up *The New York Times*. When I got to our apartment, I sat down and opened it up to the Styles section. On the cover was a nearly full-page photograph of my grandmother, headlined something along the lines of "Carol in Wonderland." There was an accompanying article about her new book, a memoir. I was surprised and curious: I hadn't seen her in years. But I also felt odd. Who was she? I wondered. I was still chilled from the rain, sitting on the lone chair in my empty apartment, and I did not know the answer.

While it was a different kind of aloneness I felt when it came to my nuclear family, it was also there with them. I felt alone when my father urged me to move out to Hoboken, New Jersey, because "that's where all the hip artists live." Didn't he understand I needed to be in the *city*? Didn't he understand that that was what it was all *about*? Or when my mother, when I would call her late at night, would say she didn't know what I should do—she didn't know if it was supposed to be this hard. Or when both my parents told me they couldn't spare even a hundred dollars to help me build this new life I was trying to create. They simply didn't have it.

But it was an aloneness that went beyond my sense that I was being abandoned by my family, or was out of touch with other relatives. There was a deeper aloneness. For a long time, though, I not only didn't know where it was coming from, but I also barely knew it existed. But then one day I had lunch with my great-grandmother.

Rosheen was an old and feisty and still beautiful woman, with a fancy apartment on Eighty-second and Park. She had a tendency to steal glasses from the diners she took me to (I never noticed, until she gave me a few). It was her background showing. She'd moved to America as a child, from Russia, and gotten pregnant as a girl of sixteen. She'd had to give the baby—my grandmother—up to foster care before she'd figured out how to support not only her child, but also herself. But then Rosheen had cracked it: She'd met and married a rich man. It had been, in her time, a version of resourcefulness. We sat down in her favorite place, the Three Guys Restaurant. We ordered, and she looked at me. I'd been telling her about my difficulties finding a job.

"Pretend you don't have any parents," she said.

"What do you mean?" I asked.

"Pretend your parents are dead. Stop asking your father for contacts. Stop thinking you have a family in California, sweetheart."

I don't know why, and I don't even know if my great-grandmother meant this quite so literally, but it hit me then that I had to cultivate being completely alone. Why? Because at that point in my life, I felt that in order to not become my family, I needed to move away from them. After that, I did.

While I don't know if Natasha's sense of aloneness was similar, it may have been. For it was a time when her parents were still going through the period of adjusting to their divorce, and also when her brother was breaking away as an adult. He'd taken to spending even holidays with his fiancée, so their link was weakening as well.

But in the midst of this, Natasha and I were together—or at least the selves we'd forged out of thin air were. And we helped each other. She helped me in moments like the one when I sat on my futon crying, wondering whether or not to become a banker, and I helped her in others, as I did when she'd had several auditions for a lead role on a daytime soap. She'd aced the part so far, that of a sassy Southern girl whom she sometimes pretended she was in the apartment, warming up for another go-see by listening to a Lyle Lovett song. "She wasn't good/But she had good intentions!" went the lyrics, and I'd taken to joining in sometimes, dancing around and singing its tune too. But then she'd begun to panic. The final screen test was approaching: It was down to just two or three of them. What if Natasha got it? Of course, as with the bank job, there was the money—lots of it, much more than anything Chase was offering up. But as with the bank job too, there was the question of identity. Demi Moore and Meg Ryan had started out on soaps, but could Natasha? Wasn't she more of a Jodie Foster type?

"I just don't know if I can do it," she'd say. "I'm gonna go to a party, and be like"—she'd put out her hand—" 'Hi, I'm Natasha and I'm on a soap'?" We agreed: It would feed into the blond Barbie stereotype that Barnard had been so important in helping her overcome once and for all, but which she found bouncing back into her life via the acting profession itself. She cancelled.

We were both waiting for the right thing. The right thing that would feel right. The thing that would make us feel we were getting closer to being ourselves, rather than further away.

That spring, we began to find it. I landed a job at Condé Nast, and Natasha garnered small parts in a film and an episode of a TV drama. For a while, it even seemed we'd leaped beyond needing each other, and one day we decided to move out of our Chelsea apartment and into separate places. "I just feel like I'm not getting enough done, living with someone else," I said. It was true. I felt that having jumped over the hurdle of getting a staff position, I should start writing freelance articles as well. Natasha agreed. "Yeah, I need quiet too. I need to focus," she replied.

But when we had moved into our apartments, things had been stunningly unfair. Natasha had ended up in another place in Chelsea, a nightmarishly tiny studio with an air conditioner jammed into a hole in the wall, and I'd moved into a spacious one-bedroom in the smartest part of SoHo. A Condé Nast friend had hooked me up with mine, and it was not only beautiful and furnished, but cheap too. It was being let by the heirs to a household-goods fortune. I could only conclude that they were so rich they didn't have any idea of what to charge. But it was also, I realized a few weeks in, lonely. So when Natasha caught a cold and called me up and said that she was afraid she wouldn't get any better with the damn outside air rushing in via the A/C, I bit the bullet. "Come over," I said. After that, she just stayed.

So we were back together, but in a better space both literally and figuratively. I still remember that apartment. It would be like playing dress-up even now, but then. . . . It was like having won the lottery. And we accepted our prize gleefully, although I still don't think we ever picked up a pan, and continued to be slobs on the scale of what another friend characterized as "bachelor-level." There were open lipstick tubes on the coffee table, Chinese food cartons on the floor, records out of their sleeves submerged in dusty corners, clothes in a heap so high I referred to it as Mount Everest. Natasha liked to maintain that I was the slob, but she was as well—to my mind at least as much, if not more. "Hey pig piggy, pig pig pig," we'd wave our fingers at each other and sing from a Nine Inch Nails song that had just come out.

But even more than the apartment itself—which was still grand, even in its messiness—it was the *idea* of the place that got us, and also its surroundings. It was in the glossiest part of downtown, and on the way to work I'd pass by all the little hot spots, stopping at a place so otherworldly and stylish for break-fast that it seemed a replica of something in some other world and time. And then I'd keep on walking, past agnès b., Portico (the store my Basquiat crush had told me was his favorite: I peered in its windows one crisp morning to find out what its se-cret was), Dean & DeLuca. It was magical, the sort of chic that approximated those *Bazaar*-like media moments on a retail level. I still recall the first time I discovered certain clothing boutiques, or shoe stores: the lines, the cuts, the heels . . . I felt like Alice.

It was a time when it felt like my life was beginning or, rather, like *our* lives were. I don't even know that I was aware of my feelings of attachment to Natasha—this identification of my very life with hers—but it was there. I see it now in the way our worlds were so intertwined. For just as we'd pooled our clothing to create a single passably professional wardrobe, we now pooled people and places and the magic of our feelings about what was happening to us.

I, through a friend I'd made at the magazine, had met a group of writers, and I introduced Natasha to them all one night. She instantly fell for my friend John, a young *New Yorker* columnist who'd taken her hand in a pizza parlor that evening and said her fingers were like one of our favorite writers', a woman we knew had once been his girlfriend. Natasha had, through class and auditions, met some young actors too, and she introduced me to that group. Among them was a boy named Carson, who'd just graduated from Juilliard and sometimes appeared on our favorite show, *Late Night with David Letterman*, as a crazed page. He was blond and funny and brilliant, and one night I remember he followed me when I went to get a drink but hung out at the other end of the bar giving me actor-in-love looks. It was amusing, and I ordered my gin and tonic and my gin gimlet "up," for our other friend Brooke, and walked back to the table. One evening not long after that, Carson and I ended up at a trendy bar called the Tenth Street Lounge making out on a couch in a heavily drunken daze.

So Natasha's and my worlds began to blend and mix, and also to fizz: The reaction was happening—*things* were happening! In certain moments, it even felt like we'd landed in a scene out of *Metropolitan*, finally and unexpectedly, together. It felt like that when, a couple of months into our SoHo life, we had our first party. Natasha was looking out for John, who showed but no sparks flew, and I was looking out for his friend Harry, the screwed-up and tortured but globe-trotting member of the literary group—the one I'd heard was always flying off to other countries and doing heavy drugs and was from a good family but didn't care. (He was the one I liked, and had ever since I'd been leaving a party of his and he'd wandered out of his bedroom wearing only boxers and, in a daze as the night rang on, said a sweet goodbye. Natasha said in that moment he'd scared her, he'd seemed so knocked out on drugs. All I'd thought, though, was: "He's got a really nice body.") Harry hadn't shown, although he'd left several drunken and charming messages on our machine. (At least, I thought, he'd tried.) But the truth was, the boy stuff didn't matter much anyway. It had still been a *Metropolitan* moment. I'd still spent most of the night drinking and marveling at my new life, at all those pretty and intellectual *people*, and then someone had turned the living room into a dance floor and started twirling and tossing girls so high that I distinctly remember at one point hitting the chandelier.

There were, of course, problems during this time too. But some of those portrayed Natasha's and my very closeness. A couple of weeks after I met Carson, for example, who remained a friend and a part of our scene but nothing more to me after our Tenth Street Lounge night, Natasha had come home and said she'd hung out with him. Several of them had gone out, she said, and they'd ended up watching Peter Sellers movies into the night. But she also swore she wouldn't get together with him. Several more nights passed, though, and they did other things: They played pool once, I think, and went to the movies. And one evening they had ended up making out at his place. Natasha told me the next morning, and I cried. I was surprised that I cried, and I didn't want to—it was embarrassing, and it also hadn't been anything special between Carson and me. But I found myself telling Natasha that what had happened was between her and me. I didn't know how to explain it, but I just knew it had something to do with trust. She told me she was sorry, and that she wouldn't do such a thing again, and I accepted her apology.

Of course, we also had more everyday problems during this time, but we were even becoming more adept at dealing with those. We had to move apartments again, for example, after our landlady came by once and caught the place in a shambles (in retrospect, it was amazing we kept that apartment as long as we did, as this woman was in the habit of making unannounced visits, and I still remember the mad rush to throw enough stuff to fill an entire apartment under the bed, under the covers, under anything: It was like being in a frightening pillow fight). But even to this difficult news, our response was more amusement than panic. We looked for a new place, and decided we wanted a change of scenery anyway (all that SoHo glamour had led us to want something more East Village). And even if the new apartment we found wasn't beautiful, our real estate agent—a boy we would lust after for months in the wake of our moving in, although we would never see him again— was, and we distracted ourselves with that. We also rallied through the debacle-filled moving day itself, as I fell down some stairs on the hurried way out to our U-Haul and, when we finally drove to our new place after midnight, we accidentally locked ourselves out of the truck. Even when it occurred to us that two girls moving masses of furniture in Alphabet City in the early hours of the morning might be dangerous, we'd been okay.

"Can we buy you a cup of coffee?" we offered the night guard after driving the U-Haul back to the yard at one A.M, and asking if he'd let us park there for the night. Luckily, he agreed—and he *was* thirsty. So we walked to a Hell's Kitchen deli and got him some caffeine. We even, in the end, got a great anecdote: I still remember Natasha, as she turned the big steering wheel of the U-Haul that night, turning to me for a second. "It's time to grow up," she said, and we both had to marvel at it: how completely ridiculous the whole fucking thing was. Our lives were working, but wow, on nights like this, they were a total train wreck. It was funny, though. I'd tell people about it at cocktail parties for years.

It wasn't long after that that Natasha's and my lives, though—our intertwined lives—went airless. It began, although neither of us knew it, one night when we went out to Ludlow Street again. I'd spent the evening talking to a group of Australian backpackers who had singsongy accents, while she had a lie-laden conversation with a guy named Sean who, once his façade finally came down, turned out to be a lawyer/aspiring actor. She liked him. They'd ended up dancing and she'd given him her number. And even as that night we'd just left, stopping at the twenty-four-hour diner on Sixth and Thompson on our way home, and having our usual, grilled cheese sandwiches with tomatoes and fries, and talking as the dusty sun came up on another New York morning, things had changed.

Of course, nothing changed noticeably for a while after that. It took Sean and her a few months to warm up to each other, and I still remember her dodging his calls because she barely had a hundred dollars to her name, and knew he'd propose they do something expensive, and she was a feminist so she had to pay half. I also recall her not being sure she liked him.

But then one night they'd gone out again and things *had* changed. She described it to me like it was a scene out of a movie. They'd been on a velvet couch in his huge apartment—

she'd never been there before, and it was one of those indus-
trial ones in TriBeCa—and he'd put on opera and leaned over
and kissed her. It wasn't their first kiss (she'd startled him on
their first date by coming back from the ladies room and sitting
down right next to him and making "the first pass," as we jokingly called it). But it was their first real kiss. After that, they
were together. Within a month or two, she was nearly living
with him.

And I tried to like him. I told Natasha, when I first officially
met Sean (I only remembered him dimly from the bar), that I
thought he was good-looking. I also counseled her one night,
as she sat sadly in a chair in the dark under my loftlike bed, and
was worrying it wouldn't work out. That evening, she said, in
silhouette, "I just keep wondering, why would he like me? I'm a
waitress." I told her that she was, as I knew, so much more. But
one time he'd come over and I'd shown him a draft of a piece
I'd done for *Interview,* and he hadn't said anything. Something
in me had cracked. I'd told her I didn't want him in the apartment after that.

Part of it may have been Sean himself. He *was* the kind of
guy who, as someone so perfectly put it once, made you feel
like you owed him money. And he wasn't my type of boyfriend.
An aspiring artist who'd taken the corporate route, he seemed
lacking in a certain type of bravery: Sean loved plays and art
shows but, I would always think as they headed out with their
great tickets to yet another one, he was the kind of guy who'd
never actually put himself on the line to engage in real creativity. He was "square." But my dislike of Sean was also about
so much more.

Because Natasha seemed to disappear when they got together, and it hurt me. It felt like she chose him over me, although I knew even then that such an idea was unfair. Also, I needed her. I didn't know that many other people, and I didn't know anyone with whom I got along as well. Who else would I run into the book editor with at midnight—as she and I had—clad in fancy twin black and drinking beers out of brown paper bags, looking like wino debutantes as we walked to an East Village bar? (Why not save money and get an early buzz? had been our reasoning, but I'd been mortified by the scene—although flattered when she'd exclaimed, "I had no idea how *cute* he was!") Who else would I spend an hour getting ready to go to another trendy bar with, putting on the jeans and the skirt and then the dress—which one worked best?—but just because we didn't "feel" right, turn around within minutes and go back home in some existential crisis about what we were doing in life, and who we were trying to *be*? Natasha was the one I would wander through the city and laugh like a little kid with, as we pronounced various signs around Manhattan with rolling "r"s, pretending we were French and collapsing in hysterics, and who I'd introduce at parties as one of the other girls we'd made up who had fruit and literary names—girls like Peach Pinter and Fig Faulkner. She was that girl: the girl like me. She was my family.

Yet now she was gone. And she tried to make it right. She still hung out with me sometimes, but even then seemed preoccupied with Sean, calling him one night from a pay phone as we were taking a walk, making me feel so alone. Soon, I even stopped taking her up on the offers of time that she did give me, proposing a movie here or a cup of coffee there. "Going from being best friends to acquaintances is just depressing," I remember saying to her once.

But I also tried to make it all right. That fall, I decided to start *Bleach* with Sarah. I'd fallen back in love with the idea of what my life could be—with the promise of New York itself— and begun slipping back into that sliver of unreality I'd always felt was just on the tip of my tongue in Manhattan and which drove me to do so many of the things that I did. So I kept myself almost ridiculously busy with that project. I remember asking Sarah if it was okay to get a haircut one evening, and being greeted with a sigh. We were racing time, we felt—whose time, I'm not really sure; probably our own—and this would slow us down. I cancelled the appointment.

But even with such activity, I felt a deep hurt at Natasha's actions, and it was a hurt that began to blend with the other frustrations that getting my own life around this time seemed to create. For it was hard trying to recover from the loss of our friendship and to realize my dreams with this magazine. It made me feel angry and helpless and abandoned. And it also, after a while, made me feel like I was heading off a nervous breakdown.

And my feelings were only heightened by what Natasha was going through, which seemed to me to have not only involved an act of betrayal, but to embody the easy way out. Because that was the shape her relationship with Sean took in my mind: the shape of escape and rescue. The shape of cowardice and disappearance into someone else. It wasn't just about our friendship, it was a *feminist issue*, I remember thinking—tricking myself into thinking, I now believe. For it was really that I was just hurt and scared and all the rest, although I couldn't see that then. No, I couldn't see a lot of things then. All I could really see, as it were, was how I felt.

So we began to fight. Or I began to incite and provoke her. Of course, I thought I was doing this in the name of waking her up. I thought if Natasha could get riled up about anything, it would jar her out of the Sleeping Beauty–like sleep she'd fallen into, where she was slipping out of herself and into some persona of being a placating girlfriend. And the ways I did this were sometimes quiet, but they were always bitter. One night, I finally did agree to meet her at an East Village restaurant for an early dinner, but I only sat down long enough so that I could stand up again. I calmly told her that I had to go to Barneys to find a gift for someone else. I hadn't planned such meanness, but I couldn't help myself when confronted with the sight of her.

But often it was not so quiet. "I'm just tired of you being so *fake*," I'd say acidly after Natasha proffered another invite, or, "No, I *can't* make it to one of Sean's dinner parties. I don't want to see him." Yet she wouldn't react. And that made it even worse. I didn't know why I needed her to react, but I did. It became almost like a mission. And then one day, finally, after I'd made another mean comment or perhaps simply done something like left dirty dishes in the sink for one too many days, Natasha did react. I'd just walked out of the apartment, and I heard the door open as I click-click-clicked down the stairs.

"You're fucking CRAZY!" she yelled. I'd never heard anything like it. She was screaming bloody murder. I smiled. Good, I thought: I exist again.

I don't know if it was right then that I realized the true reason for all of those fights and the meanness, but now I do. It wasn't for her to wake up in her own life, but for her to acknowledge me in mine. It was a way to keep her in my life for a while: Through those fights. I'd engineered it so I existed in the only way I knew how to in the new math of our relationship. I'd engineered it so I existed for her in hate, as I no longer existed for her in love. But what I didn't count on is that such a feeling is no basis for a friendship.

And then one night it all stopped. I called Natasha from the office—it was late, but I was still there—and explained I was afraid I'd gotten myself into some legal trouble with *Bleach*. I needed to talk to a lawyer, and wondered if I could call her father. It turned out he was actually in New York, in our apartment in fact, she replied. But after Natasha conversed with him—I could hear it fuzzily in the background—she came back to the phone and said he probably wouldn't be able to help because he wasn't accredited in New York. I got angry, and we hung up. And after that I walked home. When I arrived, Natasha's dad was gone, and she was leaving too, on her way to Sean's. But as she gathered her stuff up, I told her I didn't know who she was anymore. Sarah and I had gotten so much help on our project from so many people—people who didn't even really know us, I told her—that I couldn't believe she wouldn't put her dad on. She tried to explain, but I cut her off. "I don't respect you anymore," I said. And as I said it, I think that even as I knew it might continue us along the path of simply existing to each other, if only in hate, at least still in a real way, I also knew I might have crossed a line. How could she remain friends with someone who said that to her? How could she remain friends with someone through hate? She couldn't. And the truth was, I couldn't either. For we weren't friends even before that comment anymore, not really. That night only made it official.

We kept up appearances to a degree after that, pretended we were still sort of friends to each other as much as to anyone else. I still knew, vaguely, what was going on in her life and she knew vaguely what was going on in mine. Natasha even gave me a New Year's card that December that I read alone in our kitchen one night after I'd gotten back from my vacation in L.A. But it was only nice in a generic way, and I remember thinking I had no idea who it had come from really. She told me later that when she wrote it she realized she'd given up on relating to me in any genuine way. So it was over.

Yet even within that there was an odd upside, or so it seemed. Everything was less complicated now. I could close that door—the door to thinking we might be friends again, but also the door to even thinking about and missing Natasha. It was like the feelings I'd had for her during that year had slowly died within me, and in their place something else arrived. I became a girl filled with deadly ambition.

Natasha and I weren't friends for a long time after that. Of course, she was there for certain major moments—continued to be almost serendipitously, it seemed, as she'd be in the apartment (we kept living together, amazingly, for nine months or so) when I would go through something important. It would even reach beyond serendipity sometimes, as she would show herself to be the girl I'd been friends with once upon a time, or at least show why I'd liked her so much. When I woke up the morning of my twenty-fifth birthday, for example, and was so sad and in tears and didn't know what I was doing with my life, she was the one who verbalized what I'd been thinking but hadn't even had the courage to say out loud. "I think you need to get out of New York for a while," had been her simple words. In a way, they'd saved my life. Or she had.

So I would remember her, and even appreciate Natasha in the present in such moments, and I know she did the same with me. Sometimes they were much less trying moments, and everyday ones. Years later, she told me that in the last months in our New York apartment, she'd occasionally listen to me on the phone with other friends, hear the way I talked to other people. "You were really fun to talk to," she'd say she thought then, remembering our friendship and wondering what on earth had happened between us.

We both felt that way for a long time. There was just a blank, where the other had been, and I didn't even invite her to my farewell drinks party when I did leave Manhattan. She was out of my life, even as she'd occasionally dip back in. Her rare appearances didn't matter anymore; she could never make up for what she'd done.

But then things began to change. Things began to change slowly and internally at first, but then they changed quite radically one day when I called her from Los Angeles. It had been about a year since that final fight in our apartment, and I'd just done a three-day self-help seminar. It was a California kind of thing to do in my New York eyes, and the sort of activity I'd only half-jokingly sworn I'd never participate in (my parents had been urging me to do it for months). But then I'd succumbed, and sat in a room for those days listening to people grapple with what they were doing with their lives. And one of the things I realized I'd done in my life was to make Natasha choose. Choose between having me as a friend and having a boyfriend. It seems obvious and simple now, but it was something that had never really occurred to me—its unfairness hadn't, even if its reality had. Never before had I seen that she'd not only rejected me, but that perhaps I'd done the same thing to her—had given her no choice but to reject me in the wake of having been so black-and-white about Sean: me, or him. So I called and told her, and I apologized. Natasha says it was a phone call that left her stunned and happy. It left me feeling free.

We still didn't have much contact over the next several months, but one afternoon I called her from London. I'd flown to England, and would stay there through the summer and into the fall, about half a year after I'd left New York. So I called her from the newspaper I was working at, just to say hello. But I recall feeling, as we laughed and talked, a great relief. This girl knew me, and it was a sense I'd been deprived of for a long time, at least when it came to anyone understanding me quite so well. Part of it was that I was in a foreign country—that very minute, surrounded by suspendered Tory boys speaking in delectable but alien accents—but part of it went beyond that. Natasha always seemed to know me better than anyone else.

It wasn't long after that that Natasha and I found ourselves in the same city again. She'd ended up moving to L.A. during my London sojourn, something she'd been planning to do as an actor for years, but which she finally did do for graduate school (she'd opted to get her Ph.D. after her interest in acting waned). So she'd come out west to get state residency, which would allow her to attend a University of California campus. But she'd also, of course, looked forward to the sun.

And so when I returned we saw each other a bit. I invited her to my birthday dinner, and she had me over to her place, which she shared with her old New York friend Brooke, who'd also moved west, and that first time I remember marveling at Natasha's very So Cal convertible (a black, zippy thing, it was the antithesis of the "old-money, Kennedy look" that I was peddling via my '77 Volvo). We hadn't really been close, though. And one night Natasha asked me why.

She didn't ask me outright, and I don't even think she really knew what she was asking, to tell the truth. She simply inquired, one evening on the phone, about why I hadn't invited her to a party I'd just described attending. I don't remember exactly what I said in reply, but I do remember that I started crying finally, as we broke it down together—what had happened between us, and how I didn't want it to happen again. I was scared, I said, that she would abandon me, even though I knew, as I'd said that day on the phone from the seminar, that I didn't have to see it that way—that it wasn't either/or, me or someone else. But she was still someone I was wary of. So we talked about it—talked about it in a sort of fountain of words and emotion that night. And afterward, if everything wasn't washed away—all the past hurts, all the fear—Natasha and I were in the flow of a real friendship again, and we would only become more so in the following months.

The next few years are a bit of a blur. I do not mean that they come back as unreadable, but more that they seem scrunched, crunched, perhaps because they're so close to the present. They come back to me as existing all at once. But, of course, they didn't. The first thing that happened was that Natasha got to know the Bounty boys with me, and we spent certain long nights in the red leather booths of that bar, hanging out with the drunkenly cute guys—although they never appealed to her in quite the same way that they did to me. She also kept going out with Sean for a while, and he finally moved out to L.A. too, and there was a brief period when they were still dating and we all actually got along. It was surprising to me, and it was never really a blast being with him, but I could handle it. I even, occasionally, met up with him for coffee or a drink in other cities in the following years. And in a sense, it was simply that I'd relaxed. I'd relaxed about a lot of things in the intervening time—my career, Natasha, even my own life in some deep way, as California's rays had seemed to loosen me up in places that had gotten so paralyzed in the alternately piercing heat and frigid freeze of my years in New York.

And a while into it, Natasha got into Harvard—the plan was that she'd get her Master's degree there and then return to a UC—so she left for eight months. But even during that time, we got closer. We e-mailed, long and hilarious to both of us letters in which we explored that medium in a way neither of us had before. (We were too broke to talk much on the phone, but we did that as much as possible too.) Briefly, as that time came to an end, we even thought about turning these into a book, one tracing the path of a friendship over a year, through the many things we'd been experiencing. She'd been undergoing the stress of grad school, yet also finding her true passions— academia and psychology—and I'd been trying to make a go of a completely freelance writing career for the first time. But in every other way, we were still really just two young girls obsessed with boys and clothing and being strong yet sometimes feeling so scared and weak. In those e-mails, we called each other things like "peaches" and "darling," and said things like, "I'm broke like VCR."

And then Natasha returned to L.A. She spent a summer in Malibu, this time in a huge house owned by Brooke's boyfriend, and then, in the fall, she moved into a place near me in Beachwood Canyon. And soon, we seemed to be as close as we'd ever been in New York—maybe even closer. We didn't think about it, it was just the way things were after awhile, as I would call her at all hours, and she'd do the same with me. We'd spend certain Friday nights on our own, and sometimes it would be even more fun than going to a party. Often, we'd end up talking until the middle of the night, the way we had in those first weeks at Barnard, but if then we'd been in bunk beds in New York, now we were in a sports car in L.A. It was still much the same to us, though, and some of our concerns even were too. We were still feeling alone in so many respects, and we also still felt so safe when we were together.

And after that, we'd met the whole group that became Thursday, through my friend Laura initially, but soon Natasha and I became friends with them all in our own right. One afternoon over lunch, Todd had invited Natasha and me to spend the weekend with a bunch of them up in Santa Barbara, and after that we'd all been pretty inseparable, at least on that one night of the week, but sometimes even beyond it. The whole group ended up taking a trip to Utah one holiday weekend, for example, when we'd all stayed at Toby's family's ranch on a big lake and made bonfires on its shore, and the guys had cooked things like buffalo and the girls had done things like read film scripts like the budding executives some of us by then were (Laura had landed her first development job), and we'd all gone hiking through the land.

But mostly, of course, it had been Thursday itself that we'd shared with the rest during that year, and that Natasha and I had shared with each other. Thinking about it now, those nights were almost like a months and months–long version of our first SoHo party. They felt the same, in a way. Who were all these beautiful and intellectual people? I think both Natasha and I wondered in moments. But the truth was, this time around it was different too. Because we felt, more and more surely, that these people were us. We were all, as I've realized, in some elaborate and sparkling dance in which we reflected the best of ourselves back to each other on those evenings in hotel and restaurant, rundown—although only occasionally, and for anti-chic chic purposes—and expensive bars.

So it had been good. It had been good for nearly five years in L.A., and in many ways we'd come to be as sisterlike as we'd ever been before. But then it ended.

In retrospect, I can see the end of Natasha's and my friendship coming, although it was hard to make out at the time. We'd had such a volatile relationship, from our very beginning as roommates at Barnard, that fighting was never a reliable litmus test. But there was something about the tempo of our fighting in those last months that was different. It was different on my end: I was scared. And in a sense I had reason to be. For Natasha had just become seriously involved with someone for the first time since Sean—Ben—and I felt, vaguely, that our friendship was in jeopardy.

It was a fear that I tried to deny, as I was cognizant of the fact that the last time around it had led to another ending. But it showed up anyway. It showed up one night when I called Natasha, late, and she couldn't talk for long because Ben was over. I became livid, and hung up. It showed up another time as we wound down from a weekend trip that Ben and she and I and some other friends had made, and I accused her of not contributing her fair financial share by letting Ben pay for her. It turned out I was wrong—he was simply lending her the money during the few days—but I didn't know that, and she hadn't communicated it. That evening, it made Natasha cry.

But then one night something happened that made me see all of this in a new way. This thing looked like the rest: It was an awkward moment that was related to Ben, and it led to my getting angry. It was one weekend, when the three of us had been leaving a party. Ben had, in his tipsiness, made a comment to the effect that I should just get involved with someone there who'd shown an interest in me. And while the way he said it did sound surprisingly lewd—it sounded like he was suggesting a casual fling with this person more than anything else—that wasn't what hurt me. As we walked into a restaurant minutes later, and I found myself with tears in my eyes, I knew the reason was that I agreed with Ben. I wished I would just get involved with someone. But I couldn't. Or I hadn't. Even in L.A., although I'd had the intermittent fling and even relationship, they'd always been Sam-like even in the best of times—too flawed to soar, too heavy to quite levitate. So I was frustrated. And it was a feeling that was intensified by Natasha's having found someone. She'd found Ben and he'd found her, and I had no one. That's why I was angry then, and why I'd been angry on the phone that other night, and even why I'd been angry when Ben had seemed to pay for Natasha over that weekend. I was angry that she not only had someone who would keep her company on late nights and who might help her financially, but that she had someone who cared for her. And I didn't.

Of course, all of this could still be seen as a replay of the old love triangle-of-a-sort that had entrapped her and Sean and me, but now I think it was more than that. Because not only was I afraid that I'd lose Natasha this time around, but I felt that I was falling behind her too. In that way, it was different from when she'd become involved with Sean. Then, although I'd been sad and offended that she'd so swiftly disappeared from my life, I'd also always, when it came right down to it, preferred my own predicament to hers. While she'd seemed to drift into an ivory tower of older boyfriend–filled days (Sean had been in his mid-thirties), I'd felt that I was having a more *real* twenties, as I might have then put it. I was out at parties and bars,

experiencing angst and underachieving boys, having break-
downs and breakthroughs. It wasn't easy, but it was interesting.
She, on the other hand, at the tender age of twenty-four, had
seemed to retreat.

But with Ben I didn't feel that way. I felt that she was forg-
ing ahead into her thirties in a way that I worried, as I edged in
on my twenty-ninth birthday, I wouldn't be able to. For it's a
curious thing to reach your late twenties and never have been
in a long-term relationship, or have fallen in real love. On the
one hand, you can simply begin collapsing your timeline for
marriage and the rest. I did this, and at least one friend of
mine—a girl who hadn't had many serious relationships since
her high school days—did too. "I think at this point, if I found
someone I liked, we'd be married within six months," I remember this girl telling me breezily one day, and I agreed. If
you'd been sitting at the next table over, we might have looked
like two single girls who were eminently sure of our choices
and trusted ourselves in matters of love. In fact, I at least was a
single girl in a panic.

Because there was an unwritten but indelibly important
inner script that I'd suddenly come up against, and which, if I
passed through thirty without becoming a wife, I'd be painfully
departing from. Of course, I didn't know it for a long time, but
then I did. I realized it one night when Natasha and I were at a
diner just before we started having problems, in fact. We were
bored as we sat at the fifties-style counter, until we happened
upon a particularly entertaining topic: how we expected our
lives to unfold, and in what time frame each passage took
place. Although it was a brief and even joke-laden conversa-

tion, it hit something in me. I knew the answers to such questions, and I was running out of time to stay in sync with them.

So problems ensued. I was mean and angry again, and I felt Natasha was unthinking and unforgiving again too. And then, one December afternoon last year, we had a phone conversation. It wasn't a screaming or a crying one; it was quiet. What we said to each other was that we thought we needed space. In the intervening year, we have taken it. Natasha and I have only spoken rarely.

It's been one of the most painful times of my life. Oddly, though, it hasn't had so much to do with the end of our friendship per se (although that's been part of it), but rather with the wave of other losses it seems to have led to in my life. Because in the months after Natasha and I stopped speaking, I found myself similarly unable to relate to many other friends, and it was an inexplicable but real feeling. One day, I remember having a mental vision of carrying a huge weight on my back when someone had simply left a message on my machine. And soon, those friendships were lost too, series of missed phone calls and awkwardly distancing interactions. And I began experiencing a different sort of loss whenever I spent time with another friend of mine, the first girl I knew who'd married and started a family. When I watched this friend, who was my age, with her husband and young child, I felt lacking in those things for the first time in my life. I missed something I'd never had. But, I suppose, finally and most wrenchingly, in the intervening year I've felt as though I've lost someone who I once was.

Who was that? It was that girl—that girl in my head who runs so rampant through these pages, that girl who was looking for something and then finally found it. And yet, why did I lose her when I lost Natasha? I think that, although we may not have known it, we were both looking for her, and that Natasha's and my quest to find and ultimately be this girl was part of what brought and kept us together. Because even as that girl was always alone in my mind, I've come to think that in many ways Natasha's and my friendship was built on the fact that we were together in our very aloneness. The oddly *shared* solitude of our quest was one of the things that kept us together. And so we were looking for this girl. And that's why, I now believe, when I recall not only the years of our friendship but our friendship itself, there's one thing that keeps springing to my mind, and it's the idea of girlhood. Yes, the *idea* of it. The sense that I believe both Natasha and I often had that we were living out some time in our lives and trying to become some person who was almost mythical in our own heads: our twenties, and being a particular kind of girl—a particular kind of New York and then even L.A. girl. And although I don't know quite how, or even if, she internalized it, on my end it was encapsulated by that girl in my mind.

So that was what much of Natasha's and my friendship was built on—trying to become the girl who'd found what she was looking for, who knew who she was. And we walked the lonely streets of her life together. We were walking them when we, that New York night I've mentioned, headed out to a bar after having spent an hour or so getting dressed and she turned to me, looking so lost, and I had an almost telepathic understanding of why. She felt uncomfortable in her own clothes, or her own skin. But what she really felt was that she was dressing up as that girl—that girl she wanted to be, but wasn't yet actually. I felt exactly the same way. So that night we'd turned around, nearly wordlessly, and headed, in the Manhattan darkness punctuated by so many lights, home. And it was similar moments we'd shared again in L.A., when we'd ended up sitting outside one of our apartments in one of our cars for hours, the engine still running, talking about all that we wanted in our lives and our frustration and sadness and feelings of being alone, yet also laughing until we practically cried. We'd been together, quite simply, in those moments and over those years when we were looking to become the girl we'd always dreamt we might be, and even in the ones when we didn't know what we were looking for anymore, let alone if we would ever find it—or her. If we would ever find or become, most simply, ourselves.

And then we finally—in L.A., with Thursday, and even in our just becoming more comfortable in our lives—*had* found that vision, merged with it. We'd become the dream of who we wanted to be, or our individual versions of her. We'd found our place. We were still, as I'd pictured, often in those little black dresses, but now we were no longer standing outside Tiffany's, looking in on those diamonds. We'd found our very own incarnations of them.

It's interesting how you reach one thing and then immediately must start looking for the next. I suppose the specifics vary from group to group, but it seems we all have our vision of where we're going, what we're aiming for. And that quest to simply move forward, I now think, has been much of what my

leaving behind that "girl" and the events of this last year altogether have been about. Of course, it also had to do with hitting a certain age: thirty, or nearing it. Yet it still remained hazy
for a long time—not only the idea that I might be moving forward at all, but also what that might mean. For much of this
year, in fact, it just felt like I was enduring pain and loss, and
letting things go instead of letting anything new in. But about
halfway through, that began to change.

One day, I had an idea. It was an idea I'd actually had for a
long time, but it came back to me: I want to move to London,
I thought. I felt compelled to, and even as I'd always believed I
would at some point, the timing had never seemed right. But
now it did. I'd just sold this book, so had the financial mobility
to do it, and I also wasn't afraid to move. I felt ready. So, a couple of weeks later, I flew from LAX to Heathrow. I was just
going to check out Britain for a few weeks, I thought to myself
then, but I also had a feeling I'd stay. But I still didn't really
know what I was moving toward or where I was really trying to
go. I just knew that I seemed to have started moving again at
all. And then something happened.

This thing seemed innocuous and unimportant. One night,
I went out to Oxford to visit a couple that was friendly with my
grandparents, although they were closer to my parents' age. It
was nearing Christmas, and they were having a party—an evening of carol singing. It was something I probably wouldn't
have done under other circumstances, although I might have
due to the quintessentially British nature of the event: Who in
America had ever heard of such a thing? But I did. I took the
train out from London that afternoon, and I watched as the

green scenery and the ancient little villages on the way to this couple's home flew by. And I had a surprisingly fascinating evening.

Of course, it wasn't all fascinating. The carol singing was entertaining, and I gamely handed out mince pies and helped make the mulled wine full of pomandered oranges, but it wasn't spectacular. What was compelling, though, was this couple. I didn't know them at all before this, nor they me, although we'd been tied together through three generations in some way or another (the husband's parents had been friends with my grandparents). But I'd been taken with them from the beginning of my visit. The man had just returned from an ambassadorial post, and the woman—who was still quite beautiful—had been glamorous when she was young, I could tell from the photographs all around. They told me they'd met when he'd just graduated from Oxford and she'd been taking care of the British ambassador's children in some exotic place. And these days they lived in a beautiful house—the sort of place that looks like one pictures England *should* look, an ancient stone manor surrounded by grass so dewy it looks like it's been sketched in pastel as one gazes further out on it. They also seemed to have a great family. Although none of their children were present that night, as they'd all left home, there were five of them, and they were beautiful and handsome, as I could see in the many pictures around too.

So they seemed, quite simply, perfect to me. And then we began to talk. This talk began casually and informally, as a sort of post-party chatter in the living room. But after a while, the last guests departed (I was the only one staying overnight, having traveled the farthest), and then the husband even retired too, and just the mother and I were left. So we began talking on our own. I don't know how we got on the subject of her children, but I may have brought it up, wanting to choose a topic that she'd be happy to discuss and that I was curious about. Who were they? I wondered—and, by extension, who was she? So she began to tell me. What she said, almost immediately, was that one of her daughters had been killed during her gap year abroad. The tenor of the conversation changed; I felt sad for this woman. But I also remember feeling surprised. I felt shocked, in fact, by this news, and I could tell that it was still shocking to her somehow as well; I could see the disbelief in her eyes. But, after several minutes, we moved on to other things and topics, until she received a call from another one of her children. As this woman took it, I listened vaguely—it sounded warm and full of good wishes—and thought about what a tragedy it was that this perfect family had lost one of their daughters. After she hung up, I asked about the daughter she'd just spoken to. She hedged a little, but then she told me that she was all right, even good, but that she'd been in a cult and was just coming out of it. It was something she'd gotten involved in at nineteen, she continued, and she was now twenty-six.

Again, it was sad, but even more than that it was very surprising. But also again, we just moved on. The next day we talked more, as this woman showed me around the Oxford colleges in the English chill, and we ended up laughing and gossiping, almost like schoolgirls, about other things. But she had moments of sadness too. "She was the golden one, that's always how it works," she said about the daughter who'd passed away.

At one point, she tried to explain how that loss had affected her. Even though her life seemed so idyllic, she told me, the tragedy had left her bereft of feeling like she'd done anything at all with it sometimes. "But you've raised all of these other children," I said. She replied, yes, but losing just one had made her feel like she hadn't even done that for a long time.

Of course, I might have forgotten about that evening and the following day. I might have been lulled by the view from the train that very next afternoon, watching the villages and English gardens pass by once more. But I didn't forget about it. That woman stuck in my head. I began telling my mother about her after I'd arrived back in L.A.—just to pack things up, as a few weeks in I decided to give England a go—and even she could sense the subject held something for me. But I still didn't know what it was. Then, however, it occurred to me.

The reason that woman and her story have stayed with me is that she has the life I've always thought I wanted in England. She is the woman I've wanted to become and who the breaking off of my friendship with Natasha and this past year altogether have somehow been about freeing me to pursue. She's not exactly her, not her perfectly to the letter, but she's basically her. Because the fantasy of my life, the fantasy of my adult life that I've pictured and that has drawn me back to the idea of moving to England for years, has always been this: I see myself there, with a big old beautiful house in the country, surrounded by rolling green vistas in front of me and little laughing children around me, and with a bright and British husband. It's a vision I've had, the vision of my womanhood, my thirties, in some way like the vision I had of my twenties. She's the next version of that wandering girl. And, in a sense, that woman in Oxford was her.

And yet, of course, she also wasn't her. She wasn't as perfect or pristine. She was flawed. She was real. And as such, in the intervening months I've come to think that she was a sign of something. She was a sign, I believe, of reality shot right through my long-pictured dream; she was a flesh-and-blood version of something I've pictured. And thereby maybe she was a sign that I'm on the right path even as it sometimes has seemed I've been on the wrong one. Why has it seemed like the wrong one? Because the road this year has been messy and complicated, and hasn't seemed to be leading anywhere particularly ideal at all. Because, as I've said, it's often felt like I've been losing things more than gaining them.

But that, I now think, is what that woman began to show me was okay. Because she seemed to be the idealized fantasy of what I've wanted to become, but she actually was someone I might truly become. She was happy in moments but heartbroken in others; she was perfect in some ways but in others flawed; she had everything she wanted during certain periods but felt she had nothing during others. She was, again, real. And she was also the product of a painful journey, just as I've felt I've been on sometimes this year. Because although it's not as tragic or even literal as the death of a daughter, ending my friendship with Natasha—and others too—has brought me confusion and pain, as has enduring the death of myself in some way. But that, the woman in Oxford seemed to say, is what it's about: the road itself. Becoming a woman is about braving it.

So now I continue this next leg of the journey on my own. And although I'm still somewhat confused about why I've felt I've had to be alone—or at least without Natasha—in order to grow up, I have some suspicions. I suspect I was almost too complete before to *need* to move on. I suspect, sometimes, that the reason I never fell in love with a guy during our friendship was that, in a sense, I was in love with Natasha. Not in love with her in the way I might be with a guy, but in love with her in the sense that I was in love with "us," in love with who we were, what we embodied together. I was in love with being that girl. And then, suddenly, I had to leave her—both my version of her and Natasha too.

But I still miss Natasha and sometimes think about when we might be able to be friends again in a different way. One night, not long after she and I had our final talk and during a month when I'd gone out to the desert to clear my head and write, I saw a movie on TV. It was a trashy movie, and I didn't watch all of it, but it was about Mary (as in Tyler Moore) and Rhoda reuniting in their forties, and having so much to talk about and still completely loving each other. Embarrassingly, it touched me. I thought: Maybe, in the future, that will be Natasha and me.

I had a similar feeling another night around this time when I was driving around and listening to a CD. It was the *Wonder Boys* soundtrack, and a song by Bob Dylan came on. It was called "Shooting Star," and I looked for and reread the lyrics afterward. They were about someone seeing a shooting star and thinking of a long-lost friend. "Seen a shooting star tonight/

And I thought of you," Dylan began in his gravelly voice. "You were trying to break into another world/A world I never knew/I always kind of wondered/If you ever made it through. . . ." And then he went on: "Seen a shooting star tonight/And I thought of me/If I was still the same/If I ever became what you wanted me to be/Did I miss the mark or/Overstep the line/That only you could see?"

I still don't know what the answers regarding me and Natasha are; perhaps it's too early to even ask the questions. But it made me sad and happy at the same time to hear them anyway. Those questions were beautifully phrased, and I could relate. I could relate to the sense of not knowing where you or your friends are going, or how those journeys might or might not overlap. I could relate to the confusion about what one thinks of the other's path, and even to the confusion about where one's trying to go oneself. And I also—perhaps it was simply in Dylan's voice—could feel that there was love somewhere in that mix, a tenderness for the journey of both "you" and "me." Maybe, it got me thinking again, one day Natasha and I will answer those questions for each other face to face. But even if we don't, I will always think of her.

And these days when I do, one of the first things that comes to mind isn't any of the particular moments or even years we spent together. Instead, it's a whole trip we took after she got into grad school. She'd decided to drive to Boston, as shipping all her stuff seemed overly extravagant, and besides, she'd always wanted to see America, the whole country, and felt like it was getting late: If she was ever going to do it, she'd better do it now. It turned out I'd always wanted to see it too, so we agreed to go together. And we left late one night, hitting Vegas first. There, we took a room at the Rio where one whole wall was made of glass, and ate free breakfast food at five A.M. and wandered around the casino. And then we hit the road for real, and drove and drove. I found out I liked it—driving for stretches of six, maybe eight hours, the simplicity of going somewhere at once amorphous yet anticipated too, the simplicity of that kind of accomplishment. We took the central route, and stopped at most of the main sites, the Grand Canyon, Zion and Arches national parks, Mount Rushmore. (That last site I insisted on stopping at, and it seemed disappointing until we stumbled upon the tourist spot surrounding it and stocked up on pastel cubes of saltwater taffy—my favorite—and got caramel apples.) And the days were sweltering, especially at the beginning, but we just bought cowboy hats that shielded us and, as we careened through the Arizona desert, pretended we were Thelma and Louise.

We even, during this trip, tried to camp once, but we were only able to stand it outside for a couple of minutes before our fear of bears overwhelmed us—we had visions of them running up to our tentless selves and ripping us limb from limb. In those minutes, we'd looked up at the starry sky and been silent for a moment, conscious that we should be taking in the beauty of it all, but privately terrified. "Okay, good," Natasha had said to the sky as much as to me, and we'd collapsed in giggles. We hopped in our sleeping bags the few feet back to the car. After that, we'd reverted to motels. We'd also happened upon—incredibly luckily, it seemed to us—the annual town carnival in a little place called Afton, where a couple of so-young-seeming-to-us nineteen-year-old boys tried to pick us up, buying us cotton candy and suggesting a ride on a very whirly Ferris wheel, where the seats twirled around too and it went what felt to be twenty times faster than any I'd ever seen. We took the boys up on their offer, and screamed as the old-time operator—who looked straight out of a Western, with his deep wrinkles and nonchalance with his cigarette—stopped the ride at the very top and then sprung it on us that we were going to go backward. "Wheee!" we erupted so loudly that tears sprang to my eyes, and I remember I was scared I might lose one of the expensive black Egyptian-looking sandals that I'd bought so many years ago in New York.

And we just kept going. In Salt Lake City, we nearly converted to Mormonism—as we only half-jokingly told people later—when two girls our age took us on a church "tour," but we'd all ended up in what seemed to be an old theater room instead, talking about faith and God and happiness for hours. And in Idaho or some other state—they all began to blur after a while—we marveled at how everyone talked like they were from the movie *Fargo*, and then found the only nouvelle lunch place in town, where the friendly waitress volunteered to let me run across the street and make a phone call from her apartment. I needed to call *Vogue*, because the fact-checkers had a couple of questions about my first piece for the magazine before it went to press.

So life was good during this trip, I remember thinking, specifically that day when I called Condé Nast, but also in general. It was a time in our lives when we were finally making it: Natasha was on to Harvard, and I was into *Vogue*. And even though it wasn't turning out exactly how we'd expected—at least the paths of our lives weren't—it was good anyway. In fact, maybe it was better. We felt, almost palpably on those last summer days, that we were beginning to grow up finally, as Natasha had alluded to wanting to do with such ridiculousness but also sincerity in that U-Haul on that long-ago Manhattan night. But then, after the *Fargo*-like village, we'd just hit the gas again, in her little packed-to-its-gills Honda with the top down, screeching out of town. We'd gone heading into so many other towns, and we knew we would continue until we reached our final destination.

And I don't know quite why this trip comes back to me, but I think it's because its elements were somehow similar to those of our friendship itself: the fun and adventure, the moving, the not knowing quite how we're going to get there but the taking of the trip anyway. And also Natasha and I ourselves being the only constants, as it felt we always were, even in our times of distance. We were two girls right beside each other.

So I think of it now, and when I do I also think of what happened toward the end, as we got closer and closer to our destination and stopped in one last city. It was, of course, the city where we'd begun, if not literally on that trip, then figuratively, as friends: New York. I recall that day when we hit Manhattan and stopped for a couple of hours and looked around. It was an amazing afternoon. The city looked different, or maybe we were different; I couldn't tell which. But I just wanted to walk—that was always my favorite thing to do in New York—and so did she. So we did, like two alternately shell-shocked and exhausted and gleeful girls, feeling our minds overloaded with all that this place had been to us and also hit again with the reasons—the separate, but equal reasons—we'd both left it. I remember Natasha turned to me at one point. "We were so young here," she said. And I knew it was the first time we could see it, and even understand it a little.

But then we just moved on. The sun went down and that day and stop were over too. But after that New York day and early evening, I remember feeling like everywhere we'd been together had somehow been encapsulated by that trip, including where we'd begun. I remember thinking that, although we were still on our way to somewhere else, we were in all the places we'd ever been and back at the beginning too. Why? I suppose it was because *we* were still together, so we'd always be not only at our beginning point, but everywhere else as well. We'd always carry it all within us: our whole trip, as it were— our ups and downs, our breaks and makeups, our twenties altogether. And it was a good feeling.

It was a good feeling that night as we peeled out of Manhattan and headed toward Boston. I remember looking out into the Hudson River and above at the stars set into black, and then the other way back into the city, and over to the driver's seat. Natasha was there, right next to me. And yes, we were about to reach the end of the trip, but in some ways she would be right there forever. We would have made the trip, and I would remember it always, as I am tonight, from my writer's room in London, even as she is so far away in L.A. The only difference now is, she's not beside me in the car, she's up in that night sky, a shooting star like Dylan sang of and I thought about for the first time all those months ago. She's a shooting star, and my wish when I see it is that she is well. That we both are, separate yet still shining.

acknowledgments

I would like to thank all of the people whose stories—in small part or large—appear in this book. You know who you are, and your generosity in life, which shows up in these pages, is appreciated. I would also like to thank my agent, Andrew Wylie, for responding to the material so completely and courageously. Jin, Rose, and Zoe at the Wylie Agency also get great thanks. I couldn't have done it without my Random House editors, Courtney (and Ann), who acquired the book; Sunshine, who offered such receptivity along the way; and Lee, who "brought it all home" beautifully. My British editor, Michael Fishwick, also offered up great encouragement and ideas. Tom Beller was the first person to raise the bar on me professionally in a way that led to this book, and I will always be grateful. I would also like to thank my father, for writing advice that had a magical way of resurfacing just when I needed it. And my mother and my sister, for believing in me.

about the author

STRAWBERRY SAROYAN graduated from Barnard College and was an editor at *Condé Nast Traveler* for several
years in New York. Her writing has appeared in *Salon*,
Elle, and *Vogue*. She lives in Los Angeles.

about the type

This book was set in Goudy, a typeface designed by Frederic William Goudy (1865–1947). Goudy began his career as a bookkeeper, but devoted the rest of his life to the pursuit of "recognized quality" in a printing type.

Goudy was produced in 1914 and was an instant bestseller for the foundry. It has generous curves and smooth, even color. It is regarded as one of Goudy's finest achievements.